DISCARD

A Little Kid From Flat River

Volume Three

by

Charles M. Province

Oregon City Public Library

Copyright © 2015 by Charles M. Province.
All Rights Reserved.

Other Books by Charles M. Province

Pure Patton
Patton's Proverbs
Patton's Third Army
The Unknown Patton
Patton's Punch Cards
I Was Patton's Doctor
Patton's One-Minute Messages
A Little Kid From Flat River (Vol. I)
A Little Kid From Flat River (Vol. II)
General Walton Walker; Forgotten Hero
Tail-gunner: The Leonard E. Thompson Story
Patton's Third Army in WWII (Children's Book)

Books Edited by Charles M. Province

Generalship; It's Diseases and Their Cure
by J.F.C. Fuller

Published by
CMP Productions - Scholastic Division

cmprovince@gmail.com
www.pattonhq.com/cmp_productions.html

59248450

This book is dedicated to:

The memory of Flat River, Missouri.
It was a great little town before it died.
1890 – 1994

Table of Contents

The Bow-and-Arrow Incident............................1
The Appendix Theory..12
Distractions..29
How Does A Carbide Lamp Work, Grandpa?....43
The House of Wax..56
Collateral Damage..76
The Sad End of James Layton.........................95
A Day On The Diamond Drills........................121
The Great Rebellion of '62.............................148
Getting The Lead Out.....................................162
How I Got An "A" In Algebra..........................188
The Case of the Stupid State Trooper............208
Poor Little Cuddles...230

Introduction

This is the third and final volume in a series of short stories about my formative years in Flat River, Missouri.

As with the first two volumes, I wish to make the comment that I conceived the idea and format of the book, wrote it, edited it, designed the cover, edited the photographs, and did everything from start to finish to get the book in the reader's hands. If errors or mistakes exist, I am solely to blame.

My wife, Lacy, and my daughter, Michelle, continued to proof-read my final chapters, to make comments as they felt they were needed, and to generally support me in my efforts.

I've also continued with the policy of including as many personal, vintage, and "stock photos" as I can to help the reader to gain a full appreciation of the subject matter.

As I was writing this third volume, I sometimes encountered more difficulties than usual with some of the stories. Knowing that this would be the final contribution to my *Flat*

River Trilogy, I wanted to make the stories as readable and entertaining as possible.

There are other stories I considered writing, but decided not to include here because they are too personal and – quite frankly – too depressing in subject matter. Perhaps one day they will written, but that is a matter for the future.

Lastly, I will once again offer a *caveat emptor*. These stories are true, but only as they relate to me and my memory and memories become blurred and hazy after more than a half century.

Charles M. Province
Portland, OR.
2015

The Bow-and-Arrow Incident

As I was leaving a department store the other day, I noticed a couple of kids in the toy department with their parents, who were having a spirited conversation. Although I really wasn't eavesdropping, I couldn't help but become interested when I heard one of them say, "BB Gun."

I walked to the end-cap display and was listening to their conversation. They were trying to decide on a birthday gift for the kids, twin boys, around the age of nine years old. The boys were interested in BB guns, and the father was okay with the idea, but the mother was almost in hysterics. She was absolutely, positively, and incontrovertibly against it. While the parents discussed the issue, the kids were pushing, shoving, and punching each other and calling each other names.

"Those are dangerous weapons" shrieked the mother, "and I won't have my boys carrying around dangerous weapons!"

"Oh, for Christ's sake," growled the father, "I had a BB gun when I was a kid and nothing bad ever happened to me."

With her eyes bulging, the mother gasped, "BB guns are the Devil's playthings. They'd shoot out their eyes with a BB gun."

"Fine," said the father, anxious to end this ordeal, "why don't we just buy them some *Tiddly-Winks* and be done with it?"

She ignored him, turning around and surveying the array of toys on the shelves.

I smiled when she picked up a couple of archery sets with the comment, "Here. How about these? Archery is a wonderful sport. It's in the Olympics. At least if they have to shoot at something, it'll be a specific target. It'll be fun. We can all use them."

My mind immediately went back sixty some years as I remembered the "Ronnie Marshall Affair."

I was on the verge of asking her if she actually knew anyone who had ever had their eye shot out with a BB gun, but thought better of it.

She turned on her heel and headed for the checkout stand. The father followed her and the boys followed him, as they continued to punch each other.

Purely out of curiosity, I walked over to where she had picked up the archery sets and inspected them. There was a world of difference between what I had in my hands and what I remembered as a kid.

Nothing is made for kids these days without "safety" being the primary requisite. *Being safe* has replaced *having fun.* I despair for future generations of this nation.

The *Li'l Injun Bow and Arrow* set I held was a cheap, flimsy plastic piece of junk. I'm guessing the bow would break the first time the string was pulled. Even the string was pathetic. It was the type used for wrapping a package. The two warped arrows stapled onto the cardboard were also cheap plastic. Instead of arrowheads, there were suction cups on the "dangerous" end.

I looked at the other archery sets sold by the store. All of them were "safe" and none of them were the least bit substantial. The tips of the "arrows" were suction cups, Nerf balls, foam arrowheads, or leather-wrapped cotton balls. One set actually had rubber balls (the size of golf balls) glued onto the end of each little stick that was supposed to be an "arrow."

I said to myself, "Quite an assortment of horrifyingly dangerous weaponry."

For my amusement, I looked at all the toys in the aisle. There was one board game, in particular, that caught my eye. It was called *Playing It Safe*.

I read the synopsis of the game on the back of the box. It said it was, "*. . . a game designed to be played with adult involvement. It teaches safety in a non-threatening, child-friendly manner. It utilizes traffic light colors for easy identification by young or special-needs children. The spinner is attached to the board so it cannot be lost. As you travel the road of life, while playing the game, the object is to be the first one to arrive home safely. The directions booklet not only provides instructions for playing the game, it suggests topics for discussion with children.*"

On the front of the box was a bright, colorful

drawing of a village scene. Included were smiling children, a smiling nurse, a smiling policeman, a smiling doctor, a smiling fireman, etc. I supposed these figures were meant to represent "safe contacts" for children.

Included in the game were a free Fingerprint Kit, a DNA Kit, a Home Fire Escape Plan, and an AMA First Aid Guide. The game offered "Internet integration" which allowed the online creation of personal ID Cards which could be printed on a home computer. Plastic sleeves were included so the whole family could make permanent ID cards.

After reading all this, I thought to myself, "So, this is what we've come to. I wonder what the pioneers of this nation would think of this merchandise."

As I glanced back at the archery sets, I thought back to when I was six years old and my family lived at 301 First Street in Flat River, Missouri. Mama was still alive, Freddie Lee had already left home, and the three remaining males in the household were the old man, my brother Harold, and me.

It was the month of May, 1950. I had turned six on May 15 and Harold had turned seven on the May 21.

For my birthday that year, I had received a *Hopalong Cassidy* cap pistol and holster, which I dearly loved. It wasn't one of those silly little guns that only took one cap at a time. No, sir, it was a real cap gun that opened on the side so you could insert *a whole roll of caps*. To my six-year-old mind it was a finely machined tool of death which rested easily and dangerously in my little hand.

Because Harold was two years older than I, he was allowed more latitude in his choice of weapons. The old man had decided to give him an archery set.

The bows and arrows kids were allowed to use in 1950 were a far cry from the ones kids are allowed to have today.

Harold's set was an honest-to-goodness weapon. It was made of laminated hardwood. It was so strong I was unable to attach the string. Harold had to put one end of the bow on the ground and pull with all his strength to get the string into the notches at both ends. And, when I say string, it was more than that. It was a long, piece of catgut like the material used in tennis rackets at the time. Included were three real feather-fletched hardwood arrows, a belt-fit leather quiver, a thick leather armguard, and a bullseye target made of heavy, stiff paper. The tips of the arrows were "blunted" steel-tipped target-points.

I was told that I would not be allowed to use the bow and arrows without Harold's supervision. That was okay because I had my *Hopalong Cassidy* cap gun, which I preferred.

I remember that afternoon when Harold said he was going to let me shoot his bow but I had to be very careful. I was surprised because he usually told me to get away and leave him alone.

We nailed the target to the largest tree in the

corner of the front yard so it was facing the back yard. The house sat in the middle of the lot and there was a ten foot wide space on the street side from the front yard to the back yard. This would be our shooting range for the day.

We started about twenty feet from the target and I was doing okay even though I wasn't really strong enough to pull the string back all the way. I hit the target each time I tried, though. The string kept hurting my arm because Harold said he didn't want to keep taking the leather guard off his arm.

Then, we moved to the back yard and prepared to shoot from about seventy-five feet, which was a very long distance, even for Harold.

I wasn't able to get the arrow anywhere near the target. It just flew forward and stuck in the ground a little bit beyond the stairs to the root cellar on the side of the house. By this time, I was fed up and stopped trying. My inner wrist was red and raw from the string burn.

Harold, however, was determined to hit the target, in spite of the great distance.

This is where Ronnie Marshall comes into the picture.

Ronnie was a neighborhood kid who lived up the block on Houser Street. He was about a year older than Harold and they played together most of the time. I knew him, but didn't play with him often. Heck, I was just a kid and he was at least 9 or 10 years old.

Ronnie was walking up the road from *Honbeck's Market* and he decided to stop by to see what Harold was up to. It turned out to be unfortunate that the gravel road from *Honbeck's* to our house was hidden from our view when we were in the back yard.

Ronnie had come up the street, unseen by us. He walked onto our front porch and knocked on the front door. Mama answered the door and told him we were probably in the back yard somewhere.

Ronnie thanked her, turned around, and started off the porch. He made a left turn and, apparently, failed to notice the target nailed to the tree in the front yard.

He walked to the side of the yard and turned to look down the side of the house into the back yard.

At the exact moment he took a couple of steps into our view, Harold had already pulled back the bow string as far as he could and he let the arrow fly.

The timing couldn't have been more perfect nor more unfortunate.

From the second Harold let go of the bow string and the time he turned toward us, we yelled, "Ronnie! Watch out!"

Regrettably, an arrow is impossible to see as it comes at you and Ronnie began to wave at us as we yelled at him.

The arrow flew its fateful, predestined course and hit him directly in his chest, near his heart. It was pure luck it didn't hit him in the face. Had he taken a step or two forward, it would probably have "shot his eye out" to use adult anti-BB gun vernacular.

When the arrow hit him, he grabbed his chest, yelled, and fell to his knees.

We were already running toward him. We were scared to death. We thought we had killed him.

Odd things run through a child's mind when a tragedy occurs. I was thinking how glad I was that I wasn't able to shoot an arrow that far. I was glad it wasn't me who killed him. I was relieved that I'd get no prison time.

When we got to Ronnie, he was lying on the ground, moaning. We asked him if he was okay and we were delighted when he was able to sit up. He pulled open his shirt to look at his chest. We all expected to see blood gushing everywhere, but it wasn't as bad as we thought it was going to be.

I picked up the arrow and I think we all realized rather quickly why archery sets came with blunted tips. If that arrow had a pointed tip, Ronnie would be dead.

As it was, though, it was still bad.

By this time, Mama came out after hearing all the yelling to see what had happened. When I think of the things we put that poor woman through, I'm amazed she didn't run off and leave us to take care of ourselves.

She took Ronnie in the house and had him take off his shirt. His chest was already beginning to show a big bruise and the skin had been opened about a quarter of an inch.

She sat him down at the kitchen table and

cleaned the wound. She dabbed some White Mule on it and put a band-aid over it. She gave each of us a small glass of milk and a sugar sandwich.

She told him, "Now you just sit there for a few minutes, Ronnie. You're not going anywhere until I think you're okay."

While we sat and ate our sandwiches, she went outside. When she came back in the house, she was carrying the target, the bow, the arrows, and the rest of the outfit. She put them in the kitchen closet and said, "I think you've had enough of that for today."

Harold and I said, "Yes, Mama."

Ronnie said, "Yes, ma'am."

I nodded.

I never had anything else to do with archery. I stuck to my good ol' cap gun.

I think Harold ended up trading the bow and arrow set for a tennis racket or something.

A few days later, we saw Ronnie at school and he showed us his wound. The skin had healed over, but there was a very large and very colorful bruise about two inches wide on his chest. He was quite proud of it.

The last time I heard of Ronnie was in a story printed in Flat River's newspaper, *The Daily Journal.* He graduated from high school, moved to St. Louis, and became a cop. The story said he had come upon some suspicious activity in an office building on the South Side of the city and upon investigating, he discovered a guy who had broken into an office and was ransacking the place, looking for money. Ronnie climbed over the door, squeezing himself through the transom. He had an altercation with the intruder, subdued him, 'cuffed him, and took him in. Folks in Flat River talked about it for a while, saying he was quite the hero. I never heard anything more about him after that. I hope he retired safe and sound.

I wondered to myself what the woman who bought the archery sets would say if I told her that story. What would she say if I told her you're more liable to get your eye shot out with an arrow than with a BB gun.

As far as I'm concerned, I'll take the *official Red Ryder, carbine-action, two-hundred-shot, range-model air rifle with the compass in the stock* any day over a bow-and-arrow.

But, that's just me.

A bow and arrow set like the one that almost killed Ronnie Marshall. It's more lethal than a BB-gun if you ask me.

The Appendix Theory

Nothing can be simple anymore. I remember when things were much more simple than they are today, but that was a very long time ago.

One of the few advantages of getting old (and there are damn few of them) is being able to say, "Things were better when I was a kid."

A lot of people might argue with me, saying the "modern" world is vastly superior to a world sixty some odd years ago when I was a child. I disagree.

Take for example, the costs involved in the field of medicine today. I recently visited my doctor for my yearly checkup and after an extremely brief discussion of "how I'm feeling" I was informed that some "tests" were needed.

Of course, I wasn't surprised. At the age of 70, I'm used to being the victim of corporate and governmental extortion.

Per the doctor's instructions, I gave the nurse a small container of urine and a large quantity of blood was extracted from the only good vein I have left.

A week later I received a phone call from the nurse who told me, "Nothing to worry about, everything's fine." I knew that before the tests were done, but of course no one ever believes the patient. I also know that expensive tests are the life's blood of the medical business these days.

There was a time when a doctor would check for diabetes by sticking his finger into a cup of urine supplied by the patient and tasting the fluid for sweetness. Those days are long gone. Now everyone wears gloves and masks.

A month after my visit, I received a letter from the laboratory that performed my blood tests. It said, " . . . this is not a bill." It was a "notice" that my insurance company would be billed. The tests were a few dollars short of $150.

I thought about that for a few minutes and said to myself, "Things were better when I was kid."

Then I said to myself, "Things were sure as hell a lot cheaper when I was a kid."

Then I stopped talking to myself. I didn't want to start an argument.

When I was eleven years old, my appendix was removed. I have a theory as to why it became infected but I have no proof that would convince a jury. I'll revisit that theory at the end of this story after I've made my case.

It started with our annual summer-long visit to Grandpa's farm just outside of Irondale, Missouri. That would be Grandpa, Grandma, Harold, and me.

I never minded living in the old house (built with those old, square blacksmith nails) where Grandpa had been born. Nor did I mind spending the summer on the farm even though I was put to work and was expected to finish daily chores before I was allowed the freedom to roam the 200 acre farm and the large creek that flowed through it.

There were, however, a few things I disliked intensely about farm life.

One was the snakes; blacksnakes, rattlesnakes, copperheads, and cottonmouths. I don't even like garter snakes. Anything with teeth will bite you.

The second was poison ivy and poison oak, both of which were prevalent throughout the farm.

I suffered an absolutely horrible experience with poison ivy when I was ten years old. I was so badly infected I wasn't allowed to sleep in a bed. Grandma placed clean sheets on the floor of the front porch every night and that's where I slept. The poison ivy had spread over my body and I was covered with various sizes of pustules that would burst while I was sleeping. The pus soaked sheets had to be washed daily.

I have no idea how many bottles of calamine lotion we used, but I was covered with the stuff from head to foot until the my skin cleared. I looked like a large, pink pariah. The word "miserable" doesn't even begin to describe how I felt.

The third detestable thing on the farm was insects, the worst of which were ticks and chiggers. It was impossible to avoid them and they were a constant source of irritation. Simply brushing against a branch or leaf would cause them to drop onto your body and clothes.

Ticks and chiggers are members of the arachnid family, meaning they're tiny versions of spiders. They bite the dickens out of you. They suck your blood and they leave tiny itchy spots everywhere they feed on you.

It was a tick that figures in my theory about my appendix inflammation.

Ticks have a disgusting ability to engorge themselves with so much blood they can swell to a hundred times their original tiny size. If you haven't seen a fully swollen tick, you haven't lived a full life.

I had been down to the creek one day, catching minnows and crawdads for fishing bait. An evil little tick got on me and it somehow managed to crawl onto the right side of my stomach, just about where the appendix is located under the layers of skin and muscle. By the late evening, I was experiencing a bit of pain on my right side. I told Grandma about it but she said, "Quit complaining, it's just growing pains." So, I quit complaining. I never fully comprehended the concept of "growing pains" but if that's what Grandma said it was, it must be true. Grandma often reminded me that she was never wrong about anything and Harold always agreed with her.

Around midnight, I woke up with some serious pain in my right side. I got out of bed and went to Grandma's and Grandpa's bedroom. I knocked on the door until Grandpa yelled, "Go back to bed."

I opened the door, peeked in, and said, "I don't feel so good. My stomach hurts like heck."

Grandpa mumbled something disagreeable as he got out of bed and lit the kerosene lamp. He escorted me back to my bed and told me to lie down, which I did. He pulled up my t-shirt, put the lamp next to me and said, "Good-God-a-Mighty! Look at the size of that thing."

I looked down and saw a tick about the size of a dime embedded in my right side. Grandpa reached out, grabbed the tick and gave it a quick pull. It popped off in his hand, but I'm certain its microscopic head was still embedded in my stomach. He said, "Come on outside, let's pop this sucker."

We went to the back porch where he put the tick down and stepped on it with the tip of his shoe. I wasn't surprised to hear it pop and to see my blood spew into a large stain on the wooden step. I had seen plenty of ticks like this.

"There," said Grandpa, "she won't be botherin' you no more. Go back to bed."

Per his instructions, I went back to bed and the pain in my side subsided, but I still didn't feel up to snuff. I'm sure I had a fever, but we were miles from anywhere so it didn't matter. When you live on a farm, it is what it is. Complaining never helps. At least that's what I had always been told.

The next morning, I asked Grandpa why he said, "*She* won't bother you any more." I wondered how he knew it was a she.

He explained that female ticks are the ones

that engorge themselves with blood. Once full, she drops off the host and then she waits around for a male tick to stop by and impregnate her. After "having his way with her" the male almost immediately dies. All the blood inside the female tick somehow turns into hundreds of teeny-tiny tick eggs which she lays just before she dies, too.

Then the whole cycle begins anew. All those little ticks hanging around on some piece of foliage just waiting for some poor sap like me to stroll by so they can crawl onto me and suck my blood. Geez, the things you learn when you live on a farm. Ain't nature grand?

I didn't think anything more of the affair until we had packed up at the end of the summer and returned to Flat River. School would be starting soon and we had to get ready.

I had been back to school for a couple of weeks when my right side began to hurt again. I knew how wrong it was to complain, so I never told anyone about it. Eventually, though, the pain got so bad, I couldn't stand up straight.

When Grandma asked me why I was all stooped over, I admitted that I was in a lot of pain. I said, "My stomach really hurts." Had I been a doctor, I would have said, "I'm displaying indications of some discomfort."

She told me to pull out my shirt and show her where it hurt. I did so, and when she forcefully poked her fingers into my right side, I almost screamed. At that point, I was feeling downright poorly.

"Well," she said, "I guess it's a good thing we're back in town. We probably should go see Doc Jones."

The old man was at work and Grandpa didn't have a car since he never learned to drive. All his life he either walked or rode a horse. He only rode in a car when someone else drove him.

Grandma called somebody she knew at St. Joe and told them she was taking me to see Doc Jones. She instructed them to notify the old man about it. She said, "I want him at the doctor's office as soon as he can get there. We'll be waiting for him."

Next, she called the local Taxi company and ordered a cab to be sent immediately to her house at 9Y Theodore Street.

We climbed into the taxi when it arrived and Grandma told the driver, "We need to see Doc Jones." He threw it into gear and we took off without any further instruction.

I think everyone in St. Francois county knew Doc Jones. If he had a full name, I don't know what it was. All I ever heard him called was "Doc Jones." He was the "company doctor" for the St. Joe Lead Company. He was also the "go to guy" when somebody needed a fresh bottle of *White Mule*, a topical medicine invented by some long-forgotten company doctor. Used for cuts, scrapes, and bruises, it had an acutely distinct odor and a healthy sting when applied to an open wound, but it was a miracle drug. Miners and their families swore by it. Grandpa told me it was a mixture of camphor, turpentine, and alcohol . . . and maybe a little bit of witchcraft thrown in for added measure.

We arrived at Doc Jones' office, Grandma explained the situation to the receptionist, and we were immediately ushered into the examination room. Doc Jones came in a couple of minutes later. We didn't have to wait for an hour or two to see a doctor back then. He looked me over, took my temperature, poked and prodded me, and then sat down at his desk to make a phone call.

He gave the operator the number of the Bonne Terre Hospital and when she connected him, he instructed the person on the other end of the line to prepare the operating room for an emergency appendectomy. He gave them my name and hung up the phone. He said Grandma would be with me and she would fill out any paperwork.

I really wasn't liking the sound of any of this.

We waited in the doctor's outside office and it wasn't long before the old man came walking through the door. He was fresh from "the diggins" and hadn't bothered to change clothes or take a shower. He was as dirty as only a miner can be but he looked pretty good right then and there.

We all climbed into his maroon, 1954 Ford and took off for the hospital. I wouldn't say he was driving too fast, but I was hanging on pretty tight on the turns, and Grandma was yelling at him, "Dad-Gummit, Herman, you're gonna put us all in the hospital if you aren't careful."

The old man ignored her and we arrived at the hospital in one piece. He dropped us off at the front door, and said, "Go on in and get him signed in. I'll park the car and be there in a minute."

Entering the hospital, Grandma stood fully erect and assumed her "Empress Mode" of operation, barking orders to anyone in our path.

In the Admitting Office, the administrators and nurses did what they were told while I sat in a corner wondering what they were planning on doing to me.

One of the nurses took me by the arm and escorted me to a room where she unceremoniously removed my clothes, put a embarrassing, backless hospital gown on me, and told me to climb onto a nearby gurney.

I was taken directly to the operating room where they "prepped" me. The only person I recognized was Doc Jones who was dressed like Richard Boone in the old "Medic" television show.

As he watched me being wheeled in, he looked at me and said, "There you are."

Then he nodded at some other guy in the room and said, "Let's get this show on the road before that appendix ruptures."

At that point, things began to get fuzzy. There are only a few things I fully remember about the operating room, other than the horribly bright lights, and one of them was thinking, "This is turning out to be a crummy day."

For some odd reason, I remember the

anesthesiologist giving me a detailed explanation of what he was going to do. He said he was going to use ether to put me to sleep and he would have to protect my eyes from possible "ocular damage" before administering the anesthetic.

He covered the entire upper part of my face with vaseline; my forehead, eyes and eyelids, nose, cheeks, and upper lip. Then he pasted a layer of rubber masking over my eyes. This was followed with another layer of vaseline, a layer of gauze, more vaseline, and a final layer of rubber masking. A thought briefly flitted through my mind, "If this stuff makes me go blind, I hope I die on the operating table."

I found out later the danger wasn't nearly as bad as I had imagined. I guess I was scared and expecting the worst.

Finally, he put a mask over my nose and mouth and said, "Take a deep breath."

I did as he said and got a snootful of a nasty, sickly-sweet odor, which I thoroughly disliked.

He said, "Another deep breath."

I didn't notice the smell as much the second time.

I began to have a weird dream. Everything was pitch black but I could still see objects around me. I began to dream that I was having a nightmare. I was standing there watching myself. I heard odd, metallic voices and unearthly sounds from evil people who wanted to kill me. They were pointing at me and laughing. I saw Mama standing a great distance away. It was only a speck of light, but it was her.

Suddenly I saw her clearly at the end of a hopelessly long tunnel. The only light was coming from her as she beckoned to me and said, "Come here, I'll save you." I started to run toward her but the faster I ran, the slower I wentg and the further away she was. It didn't make any sense. My feet became encased in some slimy, sticky goo and I couldn't move my legs. I heard the people behind me laughing at me while they were spitting on me. Mama kept beckoning at me, saying, "I'm right here, can't you see me?" She began to cry and then she disappeared. Everything turned blood red and the universe slid into an empty, black, nothingness.

Waking up, I had a horrible, sick headache and I felt like vomiting. My right side hurt more than when I came into the hospital. I saw people in the room, but I couldn't focus, couldn't tell who they were.

I laid quietly for a minute and fell asleep again.

The second time I woke up, I looked around and realized I was in a hospital ward. There were a dozen beds but only half of them had patients lying in them. It was very quiet. I saw the old man and Grandpa sitting by the side of my bed. They were talking so quietly I couldn't hear what they were saying.

I tried to say something but couldn't talk. I cleared my throat and said, "What happened? I don't feel so hot. My side still hurts. Now my throat hurts, too."

Grandpa said, "They sliced you open and ripped out your appendix. They said you were one lucky kid. It busted open in the doctor's hands."

The old man looked at Grandpa and said, "Now, Pop. Don't be filling his head with scary things like that."

He turned to me and said, "Everything's fine. Your appendix was infected but they got it out in time and you're going to recover without any problems."

Grandpa said, "Yeah, you'll have a big scar on your stomach, but that's all. If it had busted before they got it out, it would have infected your whole insides and they'd have had to clean all your guts. It was all swollen up like that tick I pulled off you."

The old man said, "Pop, stop it. Don't be putting those ideas in his head."

Grandpa smiled and said, "Well, he asked what happened and I'm just telling him what happened, that's all."

I rolled over a little bit to my left and moved my hospital gown so I could see my side which now had a six-inch long gash stitched together with what looked like thick, black cat-gut.

"Wow," I said, "they really sliced me open, didn't they?"

Grandpa got out of his chair and looked at the stitched-together incision saying, "Yeah, you look like a butchered hog."

"That's enough of that sort of talk," said the old man, who was looking a bit green.

The old man always had a queasy stomach. He couldn't look at bloody wounds without getting a bit sick. Once at the supper table someone had mentioned something about a pus-filled blister and he had to run to the bathroom to vomit. I never understood that.

Grandma and Harold came in a little later but didn't stay long. She had a lodge meeting to attend or some such societal obligation. Harold, of course, went along to play his accordion and provide free entertainment for "the ladies."

After a night in the hospital, I was allowed to go home to Grandma's house where I was told to take it easy for a while. After a week of Grandma's television soap operas, I was more than ready to go back to school. The day before my return to normal activities, we made a trip to Doc Jones' office where he removed my stitches.

Using a surgically sharp pair of scissors, he snipped the stitches and pulled them out, leaving a small drop of blood on each tiny hole. He wiped them with alcohol and said, "There you are, as good as new."

The next day, at school, I was busy showing everyone my scar, bragging about how I almost died on the operating table, how the appendix was so swollen it burst in the doctor's hand, and how the doctor said I was very lucky to be alive. All the girls were appropriately disgusted and all the boys were both impressed and envious.

These days, an appendix can be removed as an "out-patient" procedure using Laparoscopic-Keyhole surgery, which leaves a tiny hole that is closed with "medicinal" super glue. Modern surgical instruments instantly cauterize internal cuts and patients are expected to be back to normal within 48 hours.

For me, however, it involved a couple of hours on an operating table, a six-inch incision through flesh and muscle, internal "self-dissolving" stitches, and thick, black stitches which had to be removed after a week's recovery.

That, however, is far from the only difference between an appendectomy in 1955 and in 2014.

My surgery cost $125. Today's average appendectomy costs $33,000. You read that right, Thirty-Three *Thousand* dollars. Now, I may be wrong but that seems to me like an obscene difference.

When I first researched current surgery costs, I wondered if inflation might be the cause for such an increase. I located a couple of "inflation calculator" online and keyed in the requisite information. Both programs instantly informed me that the amount of $125 in 1955 dollars is the equivalent of approximately $1,200 in 2014 dollars. So, if inflation were the single culprit, an appendectomy should cost about $1,200 in today's dollars. Why in the world, I wondered, would such an operation cost an average of $33,000? I blame Lyndon Johnson, Medicare, and rampant corruption for today's medical crisis.

Before I forget, though, I have to tie the knot on a couple of things I mentioned at the start of this story.

First, I want to re-emphasize the fact that my appendectomy cost less than the whole battery of tests done this year at the insistence of my doctor. It is my firm conviction that the field of medicine is focused on money instead of healing.

Second, it's my theory that my appendicitis was caused by that rotten, evil, tick that Grandpa pulled out of my stomach. I believe its teeny-tiny head was embedded in my flesh so deeply it caused an infection that eventually reached my appendix. Doctors will readily admit they have no idea why the appendix is there, or what it is supposed to do, or how it can become so infected that it needs to be removed. So much for what doctors know.

Yeah . . . the more I think about it, the more I'm convinced that damned tick caused all of my problems. Well, okay, maybe not all of my problems, but at least my appendicitis problem.

Above: an adult tick before and after gorging on the victim's blood. Below: after the blood has changed into tick eggs.

Two views of Bonne Terre Hospital. St. Joe furnished the buildings and equipment for this general hospital and paid for any operating deficits.

Distractions

I was waiting in the checkout line at the supermarket the other day listening to the discussion between a shopper and the cashier. "The trouble with the Internet," explained the shopper as she was digging through her suitcase-sized purse for a credit card, "is that it wastes so much time."

That started me thinking, which is sometimes a distressing thing.

I couldn't help myself. I smiled and said, "Madam, you don't know the half of it. I have a theory about that, but none of us have the time for me to explain it in detail right now."

The cashier and the shopper looked at me like I had a monkey on my back. They quickly concluded their transaction and the shopper hurried to get away from me. The cashier rang up my purchases with a minimum of eye contact and turned her attention to the folks behind me. I put my receipt in my pocket, picked up my bag, and headed for my car. As I walked, I began to refresh myself about when and how I discovered my "time-wasting theory.".

The thing is, people are all time-wasters, given the proper circumstances, and I admit I'm one of the worst. I first realized it when I was a kid and I blame the school libraries, which, to me, was the Internet of its day.

When I was in school, especially High School, I'd visit the library to research something and I'd end up spending hours simply because of my distraction syndrome.

I'd be reading about one thing and information in the material would prompt me to think about something else so I would make a note about it. By the time I was done reading the first piece of text, I would have at least a half-dozen notes about other things I wanted to know about. I would subsequently research those notes, causing me to make further notes, and I would spend a couple of hours researching something vastly different from the research material I started with.

As goofy as it sounds, I've always been a big fan of book bibliographies.

It's always been difficult for me to focus on the singular task at hand. The Internet just makes it quicker and easier to become more distracted.

After suffering from this syndrome for a few years in school, I came to the realization that I had found a fundamental flaw not only in me, but in human nature; a cause for failure in even the most well intentioned individuals.

I was so impressed with my discovery, with my seemingly ageless paradigm, I even named it. I gave it the moniker *The Province Principle*. Simply stated, it goes like this, "*Too Much Analysis Causes Paralysis.*" To this day, when I initiate a new project, I recite this principle to myself repeatedly to reinforce the nature of this character flaw.

And, so, as an astute student of the foibles of mankind, I think I may state as fact that, "It's not the Internet that causes the wasting of time, it's a character flaw in the whole of the human race. It's the insidious *Province Principle* causing the affliction.

As I began to write this homage to human distraction, I purposely made notes of the various and sundry thoughts that popped up inside my head and what prompted me to think of them.

Here's what has been happening inside my brain.

In an Oregonian newspaper dispenser, I noticed a headline about the current national debt so I looked it up on my computer when I got home. At the moment I investigated it, the amount was $17,968,371,995,300. That's a lot of numbers; almost 18 Trillion dollars.

Even as I type this single sentence, the debt has now increased by a Million dollars. Twenty-four hours from now, the debt will have increased by another two-and-a-half Billion dollars. Money doesn't matter any more, it's just a commodity, like corn, wheat, and bean futures. As Everett Dirksen once said, "A million dollars here, a million dollars there, pretty soon it adds up to real money."

Thinking about a "trillion" dollars made me think about how things were when I was a kid, when a new car cost less that a thousand dollars, when a bottle of soda cost a nickel, a pair of blue jeans cost about three dollars, and on and on.

I began to think about how money has changed since I was a kid at Emerson Elementary School, where I matriculated at the tender age of five. Emerson School, like schools throughout the United States in the 1950s, offered a *Savings Stamp Program* which was an extension of the *World War II War Bond Program*.

Every week, some of my wealthier classmates would purchase .25-cent Savings Stamps which would be licked and pasted into a *Savings Stamp Booklet*. When the booklet was filled, the value of the stamps was a whopping $18. At the principal's office, these rich kids would swap the booklet for an $18 *Savings Bond*.

Over the course of seven years, the $18 Savings Bond would grow in value until it was worth $25. Please think about that for a moment. **Seven** years for a bond to mature **seven** dollars in value. These days people pay more than seven dollars on a cup of coffee. But, like I said, a nickel was a lot of money back then.

Obtaining a Savings Bond was the only good reason I ever heard of for going to the Principal's office. Usually a trip to the Principal's office meant someone was in for a good paddling. I think today kids are given a "timeout" during which they're supposed to contemplate their transgressions.

The thought of Emerson School prompted a number of vaguely submerged memories in the recesses of my aging mind.

When I was a second grader, a new kid came to school and for some reason we hit it off, becoming good friends. His name was Bobby.

One of the clearest memories I have of Bobby was that he always wore an old leather Aviator Pilot Cap; the same kind Snoopy wears when he's flying his *Sopwith Camel* in the *Peanuts* comic strip. Bobby was proud of that cap and he never let it out of his sight. The only time I saw him remove it was in the classroom. He told me his Dad gave it to him before leaving for duty in Korea.

During recess, Bobby and I would meet at the swing set where we shared butterscotch *Lifesavers* and made up stories about being Ace Jet Plane Pilots. We would try to outdo each other, swinging as high as we possibly could.

We dared each other to reckless feats of madness, one of which was to leap from the swing at the apex of its flight and act like we ejecting from the cockpit of an F-84 Thunder Jet after being riddled with bullets by a dozen evil Russian MiGs. We landed hard on the schoolyard gravel, but we never let on like it hurt, even though it did.

The U.S. Air Force was initiated in 1947 as an independent branch of U.S. Military service.

The Army Air Corps had been dissolved and the Army was suffering from an extreme lack of qualified pilots, especially for their new

Reconnaissance and Medevac Helicopter program. This prompted the army to create a special Warrant Officer Pilot Program.

Bobby's Dad re-enlisted to become a helicopter pilot and a Warrant Officer. He was planning on making the army a career.

When North Korea invaded Souith Korea in June, 1950, Bobby's Dad was one of the first men assigned to reconnaissance duty in General Walker's Eighth Army.

One day, in early 1951, I waited for Bobby at the swings, but he didn't show up; not that day, nor any other day after that. I thought maybe he was sick and hoped he'd be back to school soon.

After a week had passed I asked my teacher, Miss Bennett, if there was something wrong with Bobby. I told her I hadn't seen him for a whole week. Her response was that she wasn't supposed to talk about it. I kept bugging her, though, and she finally relented, telling me what happened.

Bobby's Dad had been flying a reconnaissance mission when his helicopter was shot down. The army didn't know if he was dead or alive and he was listed as Missing In Action. Bobby and his mother had moved out of Missouri to live with his grandmother while waiting for information about his Dad. That was the last I ever heard of Bobby.

After a while, I stopped thinking about it. Life goes on.

A few years later, in 1957 to be exact, *Desilu Studios* (Desi Arnaz and Lucille Ball) created a syndicated TV show called "Whirlybirds," which I watched every week. I was never able to watch an episode without thinking about Bobby and wondering what happened to him and his Dad. I still wonder.

I doubt I'll ever forget Emerson School. I can conjure up a vision of every room in that old, now-demolished building, like faded Brownie snapshots. The main entry way, the basement lunchroom, the high ceiling rooms, high wainscoting with pictures of presidents and maps of the world hanging from them, block letter alphabets and cursive alphabets covering the wall above the blackboards, white glass globe pendant lights hanging from the ceiling, and the lavatories on every floor.

Oh, yes, the *lavatories*, which we called bathrooms. I suffered a horribly embarrassing predicament in the first floor lavatory once.

In those days, long before the introduction of rubber-padded play areas, our playground was gravel and blacktop and the fun-time amenities were built of steel and wood. Our wooden *Merry-Go-Round* was probably fifty years old by the time I got around to playing on it. It was not only old, it was rickety and falling apart.

During recess one day, as I slid off that Merry-Go-Round, a large sliver, about the size of a pencil came loose, knifed its way through my blue jeans, and embedded itself about four inches into my rear end. With every step I took my blue jeans pulled on the huge splinter, causing it to twist in the wound and to bleed profusely.

The other kids on the playground stood in awe, pointing and watching as I carefully and slowly walked into the school, up the steps, through the cloakroom, and into the second grade classroom where I found Miss Bennett sitting at her desk. She was filling out some sort of paperwork.

I stopped at the door, not wanting to walk more than necessary.

I said, "Ma'am, I need some help."

She looked up and said, "What's the matter?"

I said, "I have a splinter."

She said, "Well, why don't you just pull it out?"

I said, "I can't reach it, and it's kinda big."

She let out a big sigh, stood up, and came over to the door. She looked at my behind, made a face, and said, "Oh, dear, that's not good."

I said, "No Ma'am. It hurts."

She carefully guided me into the lavatory and closed the door behind us.

She said, "That's going to have to come out of there, you know."

I didn't say a word, I just stood there, gritting my teeth.

She said, "Now, you grab the sink and hold on. I'm going to count to three and then pull it out very quickly. Okay?"

I said, "Okay."

She began to count, "One, . . . " and then she jerked the offending piece of lumber out of my backside.

Her adult trickery caught me off guard and I yelled, "Owww! That hurt. Geez. You never counted to three."

She was smiling as she said, "I know. It's best that way, though."

She examined the two-by-four she had just removed from my derriere before tossing it into the nearby trash can.

She said, "You stay here for a minute. Just bend over and lean on the sink and I'll be right back."

She closed the door as she left but she was back before I could feel too awfully sorry for myself. She brought a first aid kit with her.

She put the lid down on the toilet and sat down. Then she said, "Stand over here in front of me, young man."

I did as ordered and she proceeded to pull down my pants and underwear. "Bend over a little bit," she said. I think I heard her laughing a little.

She used some of the gauze to clean the wound and wipe up the blood that had dripped down my thigh. Then she swabbed the wound with Iodine, covered it with a layer of Mercurochrome, spread some gooey antiseptic ointment on it, and finally taped a large bandage over it. When she was finished, she told me to pull up my underwear and pants.

As I was getting myself back together, I was more certain than ever that she was snickering behind my back. The indignity was almost overwhelming.

I said, "Thank you for helping me."

Miss Bennett said, "You're welcome. I think you should go to your seat and rest for a little while."

I said, "Yes, Ma'am," and headed for the classroom.

A couple of minutes later, one of the teachers rang the bell to end recess and everybody returned to class. I spent the remainder of the afternoon leaning on the uninjured side of my rear end.

After class, Miss Bennett handed me a note and said, "Take this home and give it to your mother. I've explained to her what happened. She has my phone number if she needs to call me this evening."

I took the note, walked up Emerson hill, and when I got home, I handed it to Mama.

She read it and said, "Did you thank her for helping you?"

I said, "Yes, Ma'am, I did."

Mama hugged me and said, "Good. It doesn't cost anything to be polite. Always remember that. Courtesy is free."

That night, before bed, Mama cleaned my wound and applied a liberal amount of White Mule on it, which stung like the Dickens. The next morning, the whole embarrassing debacle was ancient history.

And that was the end of it; no doctor, no hospital, no tetanus inoculation, no blood tests, no hovering over me, and no one acting like it was the end of the world. I liked it better back then. Everybody wants to be a victim these days.

I have lots of "Emerson School" stories; like the day all the kids in my class decided to talk *Ig-Pay Atin-Lay* all day long and how the teachers said it was okay outside, but not in the classroom. And there was *Weekly Reader* day when all the kids received the current issue of that terrific little "children's newspaper." And, of course, the afternoon reading sessions when I got my turn at reading and I played like I was a movie actor telling the other students a story. You want stories, I got stories.

Emerson Elementary School may be gone, but, by golly, it's certainly not forgotten.

Above: Emerson Elementary in the 1930s when the district was called "Norwinetown."

Below: Emerson Elementary in the 1950s when I was a student there.

Plastics News

WHERE can you find plastics? The answer is easy — almost everywhere. Plastics are in the air, on water, on land, and in the ground.

Plastics fly through the air as parts of airplanes. A clear plastic is used for airplane windows and windshields. A strong plastic is used for airplane rudders.

Plastics ride on land as parts of automobiles. Taillights, steering wheels, door handles, control knobs, and a dozen other automobile parts are made of plastics.

A few days ago, an automobile with a plastic body was driven from California to Pennsylvania. The body weighed less than the driver of the automobile, but it was strong. It could not be dented, even with a hammer. The color could not be scraped off, because it went all the way through the plastic. Soon, most automobile bodies may be made of plastic.

Plastics are going to sea in new ways. Boats that are really big shells of plastic are skimming over the water. A plastic boat is

Plastic keeps its good looks in automobile bodies and furniture coverings. Even ink can be wiped from plastic.

light in weight but strong. It can be made in one piece, so it does not leak. Salt water and bright sunlight cannot fade its color.

Plastics are going underground as pipe. Plastic pipe is being used for water and oil. Plastic pipe is strong and light in weight.

Plastics can even be found inside people. A new kind of plastic is being used for false teeth. Plastics are everywhere — and in the news every day.

My Weekly Reader was a scholastic newspaper published for elementary school children from 1902 until 2012, a total of one hundred and ten years. Sources claim it was purchased by Reader's Digest (for $15 Million) simply to obtain its subscribers list.

Above: A savings stamp album ready to exchange for a $25 U.S. Savings Bond.

Below: A Medevac helicopter similar to the type flown by my friend Bobby's Dad during reconnaisance missions in Korea.

How Does A Carbide Lamp Work, Grandpa?

When I first started putting my little stories into book form, I quickly realized how many missed opportunities I suffered at the hands of youthful arrogance.

I can understand how I would ignore the history of my birthplace when I was a small child, but as I grew older, especially when I was in my teenage years, I could have (and should have) spent more time asking questions of my old man and my grandparents.

I should have poked, and prodded, and been more cognizant of the fleeting accessibility of the enormous storehouse of knowledge my Grandpa and Grandma possessed. I should have, but, sadly, I didn't. I let the opportunity slip away like sands through the hourglass.

My father was seven years old when the United States entered the *Great War* which was already raging in Europe in 1918.

My grandparents were a single generation from the *War of Northern Aggression*. Their parents were alive when Lincoln was president of the United States, yet, they were alive long enough to see an American walk on the surface of the Moon.

When they were in their 30s, and were

raising their family, the assassination of Archduke Ferdinand of Austria precipitated World War I. They lived in a time when there was no radio, no television, and no automobiles. When they were youngsters, the only personal method of transportation was to either walk or ride a horse.

They were witness to the birth of silent movies, the transition to sound movies, the invention of the radio, and they owned a television. Their generation bridged the gap between America's agrarian society and that of a world power that created the Atomic Bomb. They remembered the destruction of the Hindenburg, the Great Depression, and World War II.

They were there during some of the worst times and some of the best times this nation has ever known. Yet, through it all, they probably never realized the transitions and the strides they made. They were, very simply, too busy living their lives and dealing with the small things people deal with on a daily basis.

This story is about one of those little things that no one ever thinks of any more; the simple, but highly effective carbide lamp.

I was probably about ten or eleven years old when I was digging around in a big box my Grandpa had stored in an old shed about a hundred yards from the back of his house at 9Y Theodore Street in Flat River. A box in the shed was filled with mining artifacts that he had discarded when he retired from the mines.

Among the things I found were a funny

looking cap, a helmet made of resin infused canvas, and a couple of items that looked like lamps of some sort. It's amazing how little I knew about lead mining when I was ten or eleven.

I brought them up to the house and put them on the kitchen table where I inspected them.

Grandpa had been in the basement, working on a new batch of sauerkraut. He had just finished putting the big five gallon crock of shredded cabbage into a dark corner and covering it with a heavy towel that he had boiled. Now all he had to do was to skim the film off the top every couple of days and wait for the contents of the crock to stop bubbling, which meant the fermentation process was completed. It usually took two or three weeks to finish. Then he packed the sauerkraut into Mason jars. He kept a few for himself and gave away the rest.

When he came up the stairs, he walked into the kitchen, looked at me, and shook his head.

"Whatcha got there?" he asked.

I said, "I found these out in the shed. How do they work?"

He said, "Hold your horses. Let me wash my hands and I'll take a look at those things."

I waited patiently. It was hard to get Grandpa to talk, so I didn't want to spook him. Once I got him talking, though, he was full of stories.

Grandpa spent most of his lead mining "career" as an employee of the *Baker Mining Company* in Leadwood, Missouri. After they were bought out by the St. Joe Lead Company, the mine was called "the Baker Shaft."

Many years after this episode that I'm writing about, I had the good fortune to come across a copy of Grandpa's World War I draft papers, which dated back to the time he worked in the Baker Shaft. Even though he was thirty-three years old when America entered the war in Europe in 1918, he was still required to complete conscription papers for the federal government. When I inspected the document, I was surprised to notice that the whole thing had been completed in my Grandma's handwriting. The only evidence of Grandpa's writing on the document was his signature. I was astonished to realize that his writing looked similar to my writing when I was about eight or nine years old. It was apparent that Grandpa could barely write his own name. I remember Grandma always reading the newspaper to him, but I thought it was just because she liked to read out loud and he enjoyed listening. I never expected to learn that he was barely literate. I've always known, however, that although he may have been uneducated, that did not mean he wasn't smart.

Anyway, he finally sat down and settled in at the head of the kitchen table and he began to survey all the items I had found. He placed them in their proper historical order and explained how each and every one was used. Here's what I learned that day.

Being able to function in the lead mines required the ability to see what you were doing. I doubt that many people reading this have ever been hundreds of feet underground and that they don't know what pure darkness really is. Darkness to the extent that you literally cannot see your finger in front of your eyes. Darkness which can be astonishingly illuminated by the presence of one, single, lit match.

In the really old days of lead mining, when my Grandpa began working in the mines, carbide lamps were the latest technology and they were expensive. They had been invented around the year 1900 and very slowly began to replace the old-fashioned "sunshine" lamps.

The *Sunshine Lamp* was a double-walled spout lamp made specifically to burn a product called *Sunshine Wax* which was a fuel made by the Standard Oil Company. It was made from a mixture of wax paraffin and a small percentage of mineral oil. The Sunshine Lamp could burn other types of fuel, too, such as lard, tallow, and fish oil, but it worked best with the Standard Oil product. The large hook on the lamp was meant to be slipped into a slot on the heavy-duty leather bracket on the miner's cap. For such a simple device, it put out an amazing amount of light and it was cheaper than a carbide light. Grandpa, like many miners, used one of these lamps well into the 1920s before switching over to the *Carbide Lamp*.

Carbide lamps were more mechanical than the Sunshine lamps and they worked on the basis of chemical reaction. To show me the process, Grandpa went to the old shed and pulled a tin canister of calcium carbide out of the box where I had found the lamps. He brought it to the kitchen, opened it, and put a couple of crystals of calcium carbide on a saucer. He put some water in another saucer and set them side-by-side.

He picked up one of the larger crystals, dropped it into the water, and it immediately began to bubble. He said, "Take a sniff of that."

I did as I was told and was immediately sorry I did. I said, "Boy, that stinks."

He smiled and said, "Yes, it does, doesn't it? That's one reason a lot of guys don't like carbide. Sunshine lamps didn't smell like that."

"Now, watch this," he said.

He lit a match and placed it near the bubbling material in the saucer and a puff of flame flared up. As he continued to hold the match near the mixture, each and every bubble created a tiny explosion of flame.

He said, "That is acetylene gas and that's what causes a carbide lamp to work."

He explained to me that acetylene gas ($C2H2$) is created when calcium carbide ($CaC2$) is mixed with water (H2O). The formula is $H_2O + CaC_2 = C_2H_2$.

He unscrewed the two parts of the Carbide lamp and explained how it worked.

He said, "The calcium carbide goes into the bottom chamber and the lamp is screwed back together. Then, you pour water into the top reservoir through this little screw cap. The little valve control here on top allows water to drip onto the carbide in the bottom chamber. Once the gas builds up, you can light the lamp with the little flint wheel next to the gas nozzle. It works like a cigarette lighter. The amount of flame can be adjusted by the same valve on the top of the lamp. Believe it or not, this thing can really light up a dark space. The darker it is, the brighter the flame seems to be."

I asked him, "How long does the carbide stuff last before it uses up all the gas?"

He said, "It all depends. The brighter the flame, the quicker it's used up. If you fill the chamber and the reservoir all the way, you could probably get a good light for three to four hours if you're careful. It also depends on how good your reflector is. You need to keep it clean and polished. Carbide lamps give off better side vision, too."

"Geez," I said, "that's really cool."

"No," he said, "it's not cool, it's warm. Some folks used these as small heaters. Back in the old days, carbide was used for carriage lamps, sometimes used for house lighting, and other things like bicycle lights."

"Sorry," I said, "I was just using a figure of speech."

"Oh, yeah," he said, "you youngsters have a strange vocabulary these days. You should say what you mean and mean what you say."

"Yes, sir," I said.

"Now this helmet here," he began, "is what they call a safety helmet. It's made out of canvas soaked in resin and heated in a metal form which makes it strong. Some folks call it bakelite. If a rock hit you while you were wearing this, you'd be protected. I knew a guy who was wearing one of these old canvas caps when some loose fell and it killed him. I was lucky to be about fifty yards away when it happened. It could have been me."

"By the time I was ready to retire," he continued, "no one was using the Sunshine lamps and only the old guys, the die-hards, were using the carbide. After the war, that would be WWII, everyone was wearing the hard hat helmets and using batteries for lights. Your father used the Carbide lamps when he first started out. Now he uses batteries. The trouble with them is they're always wearing out and you can't recharge them. You gotta throw 'em away and spend more money for another battery. And, they're heavy, too. Progress never is cheap."

"Do they even make these things any more?" I asked.

"Sure do," he said, "but the only people I've heard of using them are spelunkers. I guess they enjoy it, but I don't. I've spent too much time underground and I don't want anything to do with crawling around in caves. It's not my idea of fun."

"I can understand that," I said.

He said, "Okay, that's enough of that. Put all this stuff away and clean up the table. Make sure you wash and dry those saucers and put them away, too."

"Yes, sir," I said.

When I had cleaned and put away the

saucers, I took the mining artifacts back to the old shed in back.

I put them back into their box and I sat there for a little while thinking about all the things Grandpa had been through and how he made a living for his wife and his five children. It was a hard life.

I never saw those things again. I know now that I should have kept them, but at the time, they were just some old things in a shed.

I miss my Grandpa.

Grandpa Province's Draft Card. Notice how nice Grandma's handwriting is compared to Grandpa's signature.

Grandpa Province in his early thirties and on top of his game as a "roofman."

Above: Sunshine lamp.
Right: Carbide lamp.
Below: Safety Helmet.

Above: Miners wearing Sunshine Lamps.
Below: Miners wearing Carbide Lamps.

The House of Wax

As far back as I can remember, I've always been a fan of 3D. You know . . . those old stereoscopes with the thick cards that had double images, the View-Master and its reels, comic books with the red and blue glasses, and especially 3D movies.

I remember the first *View-Master* the old man brought home. He must have gotten it used or found it in a trash can because it never worked exactly the way it was supposed to. The few beat up reels that came with it were always difficult to load and they never seemed to be synchronized to give a true 3D experience.

I was as happy as a hog in slop (as Grandpa used to say) the day Mama visited the *Woolworth's Store* in downtown Flat River to buy a brand new *View-Master* that worked.

It was one of the "new" models that was square and the reels were inserted down into the viewer. The older model was round, it opened into two hinged pieces, and it had to be clamped shut while the reel was held in place. Our spiffy new *View-Master* came with some reels showing biblical scenes, Christmas scenes, the Grand Canyon, and, if I remember correctly, three reels telling the gory tale of *Little Red Riding Hood*.

I spent hours looking at these reels, analyzing them, trying to figure out how such an amazing invention worked.

It was understandably difficult for a six-year-old mind to discern, but that didn't stop me from trying to fathom the deep *mystery of 3D*.

As time tick-tocked away and I became a sentient reader of magazine advertising, I conscientiously applied myself, reading everything I could find about the *Realist*, the *Kodak*, and the *View-Master* Cameras. I didn't understand a lot of the words but that never stopped me.

Every time I would show an enticing ad to the old man I'd ask, "Why don't we get one of these nifty 3D cameras to make our own 3D pictures?"

He would give me one of his looks and say, "Those damn things cost too much. They're complicated, and you have to mess with the film and all kinds of things. They're not worth the trouble. There's nuthin' wrong with our Brownie."

Then he would explain to me, "Go outside and play."

But, I refused to fly the white flag of surrender.

After studying the advertising thoroughly, I discovered (mostly from looking at the diagrams) that the cameras took two pictures about two-and-a-half-inches apart. This measurement approximates the average space between people's eyes. It's this spacial difference that creates the stereoscopic, 3D effect.

My young, growing brain saw it as both simple and astonishing at the same time. Every time I looked at the *View-Master* or read my 3D comic books, I was ceaselessly amazed at how it all worked.

Both the *Realist* and the *Kodak* took two slightly different pictures on "slide film" with the click of a single button. Each slide would then be cut from the roll and placed into a cardboard slide-mount that would be slipped into a double viewer. Each eye would see a different image and the brain would merge them into a single image that looked "real."

The *View-Master* worked on the same principle except that it took pictures onto tiny "chips" of slide film which had to be cut with a special die-cutting device. These chips were mounted into the pre-cut slots of the "personal" *View-Master* reels.

I figured out how the 3D effect was created in the comic books I read. Two drawings were done for the same image; one in red and one in blue. Each red and blue drawing were similar, but not exactly the same. Each drawing had a slight variation to the right or left depending on whether it was to go "into" or "out of" each panel in the comic book. Although I taught myself to draw red-and-blue 3D images, they could only be termed "primitive" at best; mostly shapes such as squares, circles, and triangles.

Some of my favorite 3D comic books were *Captain 3D*, *Mighty Mouse*, and *Atomic Mouse*.

Being young and naïve, I never questioned

how *Atomic Mouse* became "super-atomic" by swallowing *U-235* uranium pills. As odd as uranium pills may sound, it must be remembered that the period we're dealing with was referred to as *The Atomic Age*. All things were possible with Atomic power.

Science-fiction books, short stories, and movies about the effects of atomic radiation were all the rage. It was "atoms gone wild" that that caused most of the mutants in the adolescent movies in the 1950s; *The Incredible Shrinking Man, The Attack of the 50-Foot Woman, The Amazing Colossal Man, Them*, etc.

As I advanced in age, however, so did my interests. Instead of reading the childish comics just mentioned, I became more interested in comics such as: *The Crypt of Terror, The Vault of Horror,* and *The Haunt of Fear*. We used to call these gory, blood-dripping magazines "headlight" comics. I probably don't need to explicate, but I will provide the hint that these comics were full of stunningly drawn women with hour-glass figures.

As the years slipped away and I reached an age where I could provide for myself, I was finally able to afford my own 3D Stereoscopic Cameras. As the proud owner of a *Realist*, a *Kodak*, and a View-Master, I made my own 3D slides. I even owned the entire collection of *View-Master* accoutrements. I could, and did, make my own personal *View-Master* reels.

"How cool is that?" I asked myself.

"Very cool, indeed," I replied.

The whole stereoscopic camera experience was neither as complicated nor as expensive as the old man asserted it would be. And, it was a lot of fun.

Having spent most of my life working with computers and with the advent of *Photoshop*, I taught myself to take digital pictures, modify them, and print them in 3D format. I've taught myself to scan old black-and-white snapshots and turn them into Stereoscope cards that can be used in the antique Stereoscope viewers. I can even turn the same images into "anaglyph" format so they can be viewed in 3D with red-and-blue glasses. At one time, I was a member of the *3D Stereo Photography Club* in San Diego, California.

If the old man were alive, he would probably "Harrumph" and say, "You're a grown man, don't you have anything better to do?"

By the middle of 1953, Mama had been dead for well over a year and we all continued to miss her terribly. Her death had brought about painful and monumental changes in our lives. Things would never, ever be the same.

The old man, my brother, and I had been living with Grandma and Grandpa Province since Mama's death.

Our house on First Street was rented to a couple named Johnny and Zada Jones. Johnny was a guitar player making his living performing in local taverns and road houses.

The old man needed the extra income and he really didn't want to live there anyway. He said the house had to many memories for him. He continued to have a difficult time dealing with the traumatic changes in his life.

All things considered, I got along well enough with Grandma and Grandpa, but it was far from a happy household. I can understand how my grandparents must have felt, having to alter their lives to accommodate a grown man and two small boys.

The old man had worked for the St. Joe Lead Company and he had gotten a fair amount of seniority in his union job. He managed to bump another guy and get a good job on the diamond drills with good hours. He would leave early in the morning and be home in the late afternoon, usually arriving a little while after Harold and I had just gotten home from school.

No matter where I was or what I was doing, I always listened for the sound of the old man's car, a 1952 Ford sedan. I was sort of like Pavlov's trained dog. When I heard him drive up in front of my grandparents' house, I would stop what I was doing, and run to meet him. I'd throw my arms around him, hug him, and say, "I'm glad you're home." He would pat me on the head and say, "So am I."

1953 was a watershed year for Hollywood and 3D movies. Television had done some real damage to the motion-picture industry. Theater attendance was at an all time low and Hollywood was feeling the pain. Motion-pictures needed something new, something exciting, something innovative, something to tempt people out of their homes and back into the movie theaters. This was the catalyst behind the 3D movie craze that began in 1953.

Most of the movies Hollywood produced were simply terrible, even if they were 3D. Movies such as *Bwana Devil, Man in the Dark,* and *The Maze* did more harm than good. Hollywood executives made the mistake of going for quick and dirty cheap-o movies with all sorts of 3D "effects." They should have been making high quality, well scripted movies, and filming them in 3D using the "third dimension" only when it would enhance the story line. Hollywood moguls never like to be told what to do, though.

A perfect example of how bad some of these movies were is the melodrama *The Maze*. It starred Richard Carlson as a Scotsman who returns to a mysterious castle he has inherited in the Scottish highlands. At the end of the movie the audience discovers that the real "master" of the castle was a frog-like creature and Carlson was next in line as his "caretaker." When he can no longer hide the mystery, Carlson explains to his fiancee that something horrible went wrong during the pregnancy of "Frog Man's" mother and the baby emerged as an amphibian. One of the final scenes shows "Frog Man" leaping to his death from the top of the crenelated castle. Of course, he falls directly into the laps of the audience. Carlson is then released from his responsibilities and he returns to a normal life. See what I mean?

There were a few exceptions to this "bad

movie" syndrome, however. One of them was a movie named *House of Wax*.

It was a remake of the 1933 movie *Mystery of the Wax Museum* directed by Michael Curtiz and starring Lionel Atwill and Fay Wray (from King Kong fame). It was also the last Hollywood film to use the "two-color process" which was replaced that same year by the new, amazing, and stupendous Technicolor process.

Mystery of the Wax Museum is also a wonderful example of Art Deco, 1930s fashions, and "streamline" architecture.

Other than being filmed in 3D, *House of Wax* held a few other significant bits of trivia. It was the first movie Vincent Price did in the horror genre. Prior to this, he was just one of many film actors and it was this movie that started his career as a "horror star." The movie also introduced an actor named Charles Buchinsky as the mute assistant. In his next movie, however, he would change his name to Charles Bronson.

I had seen previews of the movie at the Roseland Theater and I had been scouring the newspapers to find out when it would play in Flat River. I was really, really looking forward to seeing it. When I discovered that it was scheduled to grace the Roseland's silver screen during the summer of 1953, I was both disappointed and disheartened.

Grandpa and Grandma always packed up and left the house in Flat River for the summer. From the end of the school year to be start of the school year, we all (except for the old man) spent the summer on Grandpa's farm near the small town of Irondale, living in the house where Grandpa was born in 1885.

My despondency and melancholia got the better of me. I felt so bad about this catastrophic turn of events that I went to the old man and told him about the horrible obstacle thrown in my face by the evil fates. He said he would "think about it" and I knew what that meant. It was Adult Talk meaning "don't bother me."

I was not to be deterred, however. I took my case to Grandpa who sent me to Grandma and I began to realize there would be no reprieve from this atrocity inflicted upon me. I resigned myself to the fact that I would never see the *House of Wax.* I was morose, to say the least.

And then, an amazing thing happened. Something I had never expected. About a week before we were getting ready to move to the farm for the summer, I ran out to meet the old man and he said, "I think you might be able to see that 3D movie you're so whiny about."

I couldn't believe my ears. I was stunned. I almost fell over. Could it be that I'd really be able to see a 3D movie? A 3D movie in Technicolor? A 3d Movie in Technicolor with Vincent Price and things flying right off the screen and into my lap?

"What's the plan?" I said, wide-eyed and wondering.

"Well," he began, "I guess I could drive out on a Saturday morning, pick you up, and we could drive back to town in time for the matinee. It'll still be daylight when the show's over and I can take you back to the farm. You think you can stand all that driving?"

His question about me being able to "stand all the driving" was in reference to my horrible tendency toward getting car-sick.

I gritted my teeth, thought of the possible consequences, and said, "Yes, sir. You betcha I can. If I have to, I'll hang my head out the window all the way. I promise not to puke in the car. Can we do it? Please?"

Much to my relief, he actually smiled a little and said, "Okay, if you think you can handle it."

I hugged him again, and said, "Thank you! This is gonna be so much fun."

For the next few weeks I was as good as gold. I wasn't about to do anything to jeopardize my chances for seeing *House of Wax* . . . in 3D! I didn't even mind all the preparation, the moving, and the remoteness of Grandpa's farm once we got there for the summer.

After the weeks, days, hours, and minutes of waiting, *the* Saturday had arrived. I got up early, did my chores, and got ready. I grabbed a couple of paper bags and slipped them in my back pocket just in case I needed them for a possible "accident" in the car.

The plan was for the old man to get to the farm around noon so we could make the matinee. I tried not to watch the clock as the time approached. The minute hand seemed to move with glacial speed.

From the screened-in front porch of the old farmhouse, I sat and watched the road that wound up the hill to the left about two miles away. Even that far away, it was possible to see the dust trail made by a car coming down the road. Or, as we used to call it, Province Road. There were so many Province farms along that stretch of road from Irondale to Potosi people had always called it Province Road.

I watched the clock hands move close to 12:00, right onto 12:00, and then past 12:00. The old man hadn't made it on time. I began to wonder. There was still time, though, I thought to myself, trying to put a positive spin on the situation.

One o'clock came and went.

Two o'clock came and went.

I sat on the porch and wondered what in the world might have happened. I worried that the old man might have been in an accident or something terrible might have happened to him.

When I had just about given up and as the hands of the old windup Westclox approached three o'clock, I saw a dust trail starting over the hill and began to hope that it was the old man. I watched the dust cloud move toward our farm road and I was able to make out the car making the right turn toward the old farmhouse. It was the old man's '52 Ford.

There was still time, I told myself. Maybe he had car trouble or something. I tried to make myself believe that we could still make it for the first evening performance and we could be back to the farm around dark. No problem, it's going to be okay. I tried to convince myself, but I was still sorely disappointed. I went out to the gate and waited.

The maroon Ford roared up the road and turned into the small patch of grass next to the gate and when the old man got out, I walked over to him and gave him the usual hug.

"Is everything okay?" I asked. "We can still make the movie, can't we?"

"Let's go inside," he said. He was as non-committal as a hostile witness on a Perry Mason re-run. I stood and watched him go inside the house carrying a paper bag.

I didn't really want to, but I went inside, too.

Grandma, Grandpa, Harold, and the old man were all sitting in the front room, talking. I never said a word as I sat down in a rickety old chair in the corner of the room. Both Grandma and Grandpa watched me. The old man pretty much ignored me.

After a few pleasantries, the old man opened the paper bag he had carried inside with him. "This is for you," he said. I got up, walked over and took the toy he handed to me. I gave it a cursory glance and wondered why he bothered. It was one of those "paddle-balls" with the rubber ball attached to the paddle by a long rubber band which was stapled onto the paddle. The paddle had the words "House of Wax" stamped in the middle of it. I think it cost all of ten cents.

I knew what it was. At the opening of the

House of Wax, there was a guy with a similar paddle smacking the ball into the sacrosanct "fourth wall" of the movie screen, directly into the faces of the audience. It was a cheesy way to introduce 3D special effects. The cashiers at the Roseland Theater were selling them at the ticket booth.

I was unimpressed, but, I had been brought up to be polite, so I simply said, "Thanks," and sat returned to the chair in the corner.

Then he took a pair of red-and-blue cardboard glasses out of the bag. It had *House of Wax* printed on both outside parts of the ear-pieces. He handed the glasses to Harold and said, "How about that?" Harold said, "Thank you," and put the glasses on the table next to him. I have no idea what he expected my brother to do with them. Harold didn't even care about 3D.

Grandma looked at Grandpa and raised her eyebrows. Grandpa looked at me, looked at the old man, and he just shook his head. Neither one spoke a word. That's when the old man started his "explanation."

Apparently he had come into the changing room at the Federal Hill mine a few days ago and he met his pal, Finis Cunningham. They got to talking and he mentioned his plan to take me to see the *House of Wax*. When Finis heard that, he said, "Ya know, I bin wantin' ta see that there movie,too. How 'bout we go see together this Friday night. I'll bring the little woman and you kin bring yer girl friend. It oughta be a hoot."

The old man explained that Finis had even offered to pay for the tickets and he couldn't pass up a bargain like that. He said since he had already seen it, he didn't want to see it again. He said he knew I'd understand and after all, he did bring me the paddle-ball.

I said, "Yes, sir, I understand. Thank you for the paddle-ball."

I spoke directly to Grandma, "I need to go outside and do something. May I be excused, please?"

Grandma said, "Of course," and I went outside.

I walked the quarter-mile down the path to the spring, got a drink with the little gourd that was hung on a stick next to it, and then stepped across the large rocks in the creek to get to the other side.

I sat down on the edge of the creek and watched the minnows, the tadpoles, and the crawdads. I have no idea how long I was there, but when the sun was started to go behind the trees lining the creek, I got up to go back to the farmhouse.

I walked back up the spring path, and stopped when I got close enough to see the house. The old man's car was gone and everything was as quiet as a summer evening can be on a farm. A mockingbird was singing somewhere in the woods and I heard some squirrels chattering to each other.

I continued up the path, went into the house, and I noticed that the 3D glasses and paddle-ball were both lying on top of the big Philco radio against the wall.

Grandma and Grandpa were out on the front porch. Grandma was shelling peas and Harold was helping her. Grandpa had his harmonica out and was quietly playing *Red Wing*:

The moon shines tonight on pretty Red Wing
The breeze is sighing, the night bird's crying,
For afar 'neath his star her brave is sleeping,
While Red Wing's weeping her heart away.

Grandma looked up, smiled, and said, "Are you okay, Mike?"

I smiled back and said, "Yes, ma'am. I'm just fine."

Grandpa winked at me.

As a thought flickered through my mind, I said, "I'll be right back."

"Don't be too long. Supper'll be ready soon," said Grandma.

"Yes, ma'am, I'll be quick, it won't take long," I acknowledged.

As I went by the radio, I picked up the paddle-ball and ambled the hundred yards down to the old out-house. I stood at the door for a few moments and then went inside. I pulled the rubber ball off the rubber band and pulled the rubber band off the paddle. I dropped all three into hole number one.

I started back to the farmhouse since I had promised Grandma I'd be quick about my business. I went in and turned on the radio hoping to hear *The Green Hornet* or maybe *Fibber McGee and Molly.*

Epilog

Many years later, I had the opportunity to see *The House of Wax.* It was on the late, late show one night so I taped it on our Betamax VCR.

After watching it, I wondered why in the world I made such a fuss over it. Other than being in 3D, it was simply a poor remake of *The Mystery of the Wax Museum.*

If the old man were still alive, I would most certainly make a point of apologizing to him for the whole episode. As a kid, though, I often forgot that people have lives of their own.

By the way, here's a bit of trivia about the movie: the director, a guy named Andre De Toth only had one good eye. During the daily rushes, he had to keep asking his cast and crew if the 3D effects worked properly. Go figure.

Above: Stereoscope and Stereocards
from the 1860s to the 1920s

Below: Viewmaster viewers; 1930s model
on the left and 1940s model on the right.

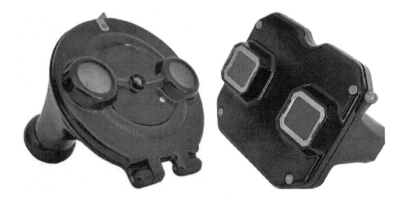

Top-to-Bottom: Kodak, Realist, and Viewmaster stereo cameras.

Buying Tickets for 3-D Picture, "Man in the Dark"

Above is shown the crowd at Roseland Theatre Sunday afternoon in line buying tickets for the new 3 Dimension Picture, "Man in the Dark." The movie has been running all week and showing to a full house at each performance. It is something new in the entertainment field and very interesting. The theatre management hopes to be able to have another 3-D picture sometime in June, which will be "4-Ti."

—Knepper Photo

Before Indiana Jones, Toy Story, Star Wars, and Harry Potter, there was . . .

3D!

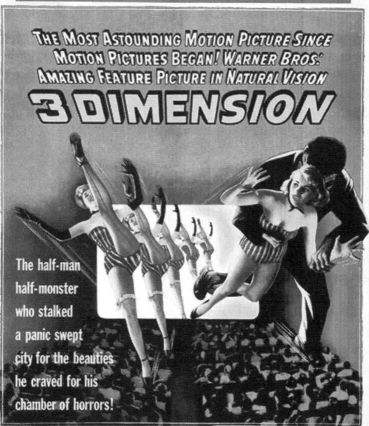

Collateral Damage

Mining is a dangerous occupation. Being careful is imperative to living through a shift in the mines, but being careful doesn't always preclude the possibility of being seriously injured or being killed.

The earliest recorded death I could find in the Lead Belt mines was the death of William Cape in 1872. He was killed when five tons of "loose" fell on him.

The last reported death was in 1971, a year before mining operations ceased in the Lead Belt when Hershel L. Daugherty, fell from a sixty-foot high trapeze.

Between 1872 and 1971, there were hundreds of deaths in the lead mines and they came in an astonishingly varied number of ways. Most injuries and deaths occurred from loose falling on miners, from train accidents, mishandling of explosives, and falls from trapeze. But, every now and then, a freak accident took place that would defy logic.

For example, one man was entering the shaft cage to be hoisted to the top when a large piece of ice broke loose from the hoist and fell on his head. Perhaps the oddest accident occurred in 1899 when Sam Downes was killed at Crawley

Shaft in the Crawley Bottom section of Flat River. A large hog had been rooting around when it slipped and fell into the shaft, falling directly onto Sam's head. Both Sam and the hog were killed.

In 1958, my old man became a mining statistic. He was operating a skip loader when a large piece of ore shifted and caused the loader to slip onto its side against a pillar. The problem was that the old man was between the pillar and the skip loader. We later made jokes about the accident saying, "He was between a rock and a hard place, literally."

Of course, at the time it happened we weren't joking. The guy who found him thought he was dead and he took his time getting help. Luckily, when the ambulance brought him to the Bonne Terre Hospital, there was a team of doctors who knew what to do. He had been crushed from the shoulders to the waist. The doctors said his rib cage had been busted into pieces and they were surprised to find his spine fully intact. They said for a man to have suffered the damage he had, he was very lucky. Once he healed, they said, he should be able to walk normally.

The surgeons later explained to us (Grandpa, Grandma, Harold, and me) that small, broken pieces of each rib had to be wired together to keep them in place until the bones knitted together. It was a long, painstaking process and the old man was on the operating table for hours. Until the day he died, he still had dozens of those little pieces of wire inside him. Both of his shoulders were cracked and separated but the surgeons were able to patch them back together so they worked properly.

The old man's right shoulder developed problems during the healing process and for a long time it lacked the full range of motion that it should have had. He could barely raise his arm. Throughout his recovery, I worked with him on his physical therapy, trying to get that shoulder to move correctly. Finally, one day, when I was getting tired of the daily ritual, I forced his arm up a lot further than I probably should have and we heard a very loud "pop" inside his shoulder. He screamed, jerked his arm downward, and stood there muttering a few choice profanities.

We were both very much surprised at the next therapy session. He began to move the arm and the shoulder worked without the slightest problem. The old man said, "Well, hell, who would-a thunk it."

We always joked about that afterwards. I would say, "No pain," and he would say, "No gain." The truth, however, was that the old man was never the same after his accident. He eventually took an early retirement from the mines and spent a few years as a Deputy Sheriff when Ken Buckley was Sheriff of St. Francois County.

I have a few stories about those years, but they'll have to wait.

It wasn't always miners who suffered horrible misadventures. There's one particular accident that comes to mind involving three young boys who lived in Desloge, Missouri.

I had forgotten about it until my nephew, John Province, emailed me one day asking what I knew about it. He said he had heard rumors many, many years ago and he wondered if I could confirm the veracity of the story. I was only nine years old when it happened, so it didn't register well with me at the time, but I did remember it. Because of John's inquiry, I decided to reacquaint myself with the facts of the case.

I remember the St. Joe Lead Company making a point of sending "safety instructors" to all the schools in the Lead Belt to warn everyone about the dangers of blasting caps, dynamite, fuses, and any sort of explosive in general. We were shown examples of these dangerous explosive devices with the admonition, "If you find any of these, don't touch them. Contact an adult immediately."

I thought it was odd because every year I was allowed to buy fireworks of various types that were as powerful as a blasting cap, if not more so. Things like *Cherry Bombs*, *Silver Salutes*, and *M60s* to name a few. They weren't anything like a stick of dynamite, but all of them were capable of blowing your hand off.

The victims of the accident were Hubert Prather, 16, Lem Webb, 17, and Leeman Webb, 13. All three boys were from Desloge and all three died instantly on January 3, 1953.

Hubert Dale Prather, born on July 5, 1937,

was the fourth youngest of nine children of Perry and Maggie Bailey Prather. His six brothers and two sisters were Perry of Mineral Point, Curtis of Elvins, Mrs. Wilma Coleman of DeSoto, and Delbert, Burlin, Jimmie, Wayne, and Mildred who lived at home. Hubert's Funeral services were held at the Church of God in Gumbo with Reverend John Rider officiating. Internment was in Mitchell Cemetery. The Prather family lived on a farm near Desloge.

Lem Thomas Webb was born on May 11, 1935. His younger brother, *Leeman Bryan Webb*, was born on January 19, 1937. The boys' parents were Steve and Roxie Leftridge Webb. Their three sisters and one brother were Mrs. Paul Coppedge, of Jalon, California; and Lavern, Linda, and Larry who lived at home. Two brothers and one sister had preceded them in death. Their joint funeral services were held at the East Bonne Terre Baptist Church, with Reverend Darrell Thompson officiating. Internment was in the St. Francois Memorial Cemetery. The Webb family had just moved into the house in Desloge a few weeks prior to the accident. Mr. Webb was a warehouse watchman for the Bonne Terre Farming and Cattle Company, a holding company owning the St. Joseph Lead Company.,

On the morning of the incident, Lem Webb had just finished his milking chores in the family's barn. He handed the milk pail to an uncle and told him that he and his brother, Leeman, were "going shooting" with Hubert

Prather.

The "shooting practice" was to take place in the field near their house. It was an irregular shaped, thirty-five acre piece of land bordering Cantwell on the north and Desloge on the northwest and west. A public highway and railroad also ran parallel to the field on the western side.

Located on the acreage was a powder house magazine near the old National No. 3 mine shaft. It had been used by the National Lead Company to store dynamite before the company was bought out by St. Joe. The building went unused for a few years, but in 1951, St. Joe began to store blasting caps there.

When the accident occurred, there were approximately 300,000 blasting caps in the magazine which was about a six-month supply. That many blasting caps could be used to set off enough dynamite to break about 1,500,000 tons of rock. The caps were packed in cartons which were placed on oak racks about five feet tall.

This is where facts and answers don't exist. No one will ever know with absolute certainty what happened that day. The only three witnesses to the horrendous explosion were killed instantly.

The theory was that the boys were shooting at the steel door of the magazine and somehow they caused the explosion, but no one could prove it. No one believed that the blasting caps in the magazine simply exploded spontaneously, but, no one could prove that either.

A few days after the catastrophe, an inquest was held by Coroner Bill Miller. None of the witnesses' testimony could offer any solid evidence as to what caused the explosion. The Coroner's Jury quickly returned an "open" verdict with the statement that, "The deceased came to their deaths by an explosion of dynamite caps."

What is known is that the explosion was so powerful it rocked the countryside for miles around the Lead Belt.

The measurements of the powder house magazine was twelve-feet by twenty-feet with ten-foot high walls. There were three ventilators in the sides and one in the roof, all of which were protected by heavy screen mesh over the openings. The only other opening to the building was the door, constructed of three-eights of an inch steel plate with inch thick plywood on the inside of the door. The door had a "safety lock" that only went halfway through and required two keys to operate.

The explosion that literally blew the building to pieces, was violent enough to cause injuries to nearby houses in Desloge and Cantwell. The concussion from the blast shook houses, broke window glass, and cracked walls inside some of the houses.

The force of the explosion hurled the 300 pound steel door nearly 700 feet. The broken stock of the .22 rifle was found 40 feet from the door and the rifle's barrel was found 20 feet from the body of one of the boys.

Electric power in the area was interrupted for a few minutes when the steel door slammed into a power line 500 feet away.

The building, itself, was broken into concrete chunks weighing between half-a-pound to 300 pounds. One of the largest chunks was thrown with enough force to smash through Paul Black's business office 150 feet from the scene. Virgil Adams, of Flat River, was at his farm 35 miles from the site when he heard the blast and felt the concussion. He thought it might have been a train wreck on the Missouri-Pacific railroad line.

Compounding the problems of the situation was the fact that within minutes sightseers began to show up on the scene of the disaster. Some people in the crowd were taking pictures of the boys' dead bodies while others were picking through the debris for souvenirs. Traffic in the area became snarled within a few minutes throughout the town.

A St. Joe Safety Department Team arrived as soon as possible to scatter the crowd and get traffic moving again. Thousands of unexploded blasting caps were littered over the property and many ghoulish gawkers were picking them up as souvenirs of the grim proceedings, not caring that they were highly explosive and extremely dangerous.

On the following Sunday, large numbers of people drove by the damaged site, trying to get a view of the destruction, but by then St. Joe had roped off the area and assigned special watchmen to prevent the public from entering the property. I often wonder what it is about people that intrigues them to enjoy a show of death and destruction.

During the week, company employees had been scouring the area and gathering the unexploded caps that could be found. On Monday, at least forty bales of straw were saturated with fuel oil and set afire with the hope that any remaining, stray caps would be set off. On Thursday, a huge caterpillar and dozens of trucks appeared on the scene to cover the area with thousands of tons of chat.

St. Joe made a plea through the newspapers and radio stations, asking people to contact the company if they had blasting caps in their possession. The company offered to come to their homes, pick up the explosive devices, and no questions would be asked.

At this point in my investigations, I began to have questions of my own, but not specifically about the explosion or the cause of it.

As could be expected, a lawsuit was filed against St. Joe.

The Prather family filed a suit claiming damages for Hubert's death, "... caused by an explosion of dynamite blasting caps owned by the St. Joseph Lead Company and stored in a magazine building located on land owned by the defendant in Missouri." The lawsuit additionally claimed that the powder house, and its use, constituted a public nuisance and negligence.

I was unable to find any evidence that the

Webb family filed a lawsuit for the deaths of Lem and Leeman. It occurred to me that since Mr. Webb was an employee of the *Bonne Terre Farming and Cattle Company* (essentially the same corporate entity as St. Joe) he may have been offered a separate settlement by the company. If such a deal was made, there was most probably a requirement that the Webb family never discuss such a settlement. This, however, is pure conjecture on my part. I found no evidence of any such bargain.

Nor, did I find any indication of a settlement offer to the Prather family. If such a settlement was offered, it was certainly insufficient to preclude the family from suing St. Joe.

The lawsuit went before a judge and jury and the St. Joseph Lead Company was found guilty of, " . . . negligence by maintaining an attractive nuisance in an area where children were known to play and townspeople had used the field as a thoroughfare."

The irony of the guilty verdict was that the jury said it was St. Joe's responsibility to prove the boys were trespassing and the only way to prove trespassing was to prove that they had, in fact, caused the explosion by shooting the .22 rifle at the powder house. But, because the only witnesses to the event were the boys themselves and they were all dead, it was impossible to prove the exact cause of the explosion.

After some consideration, I came to the conclusion that St. Joe should have offered the additional possibility that the rifle could have been used to shoot through the heavy mesh on the sides of the magazine. Admittedly, that concept would not be absolute proof, but it would seem much more plausible, and make a lot more sense, than a .22 bullet being able to go through a steel door three-eighths of an inch thick. It may have given the jury enough "reasonable doubt" to find in their favor. But, again, that's purely conjecture on my part.

Had the company been able to provide verifiable proof that the boys were responsible for the explosion, it would have won the lawsuit.

It was an odd, *Catch-22* situation. Everyone *knew* the boys had been shooting at the magazine full of blasting caps, but no one could prove it, therefore St. Joe was responsible.

Of course, St. Joe was far from blameless. They were culpable in many ways when it came to the trespass issue.

It was no surprise that St. Joe appealed the jury's decision. That's what large corporations do. It keeps their lawyers busy.

St. Joe pleaded the case that Hubert, Lem, and Leeman were, " . . . jointly engaged in discharging firearms and . . . they entered upon said property and discharged firearms thereon without the knowledge, permission, or consent of the defendant, and were trespassers . . ." The company was hoping the Circuit Court would be more lenient in their claims of trespass.

The appeal was heard before Missouri Circuit Court judges Stone, Johnson, and Vogel. Judge Stone wrote the judicial opinion on November

13, 1956. Here is a summation of that opinion:

" . . . we find that the defendant knowingly permitted a powder magazine to stand in disuse for many years in an open field that was much traveled and used by the public, and near a public road and a private road. The public had made paths across the field by their use. The defendant had constructed stiles for the public to cross over the fences into the fields. The tract was not entirely fenced. Children were known to play in the field and about and on the powder magazine when it was in disuse. Men trained their dogs in the field and discharged firearms.

Only at the extreme northwest corner were any signs posted indicating the defendant's objection to use of the field by the public. The signs were posted where a private wagon road entered the field.

Residences were within two hundred yards of the powder magazine. It was from one of the homes so situated that the deceased, joining with companions who lived in the home, started on the venture that resulted in his death.

The field in which the powder magazine was located adjoined two villages. Under these conditions, and with these surrounding circumstances, the defendant renovated the powder house and placed a large quantity of dynamite caps in boxes in the house. The boxes were piled on runners to a height of about five feet.

Thereafter the defendant made no effort to

warn those it knew were using the tract of land of the presence of explosives in the powder magazine. It neither fenced the magazine nor posted notice of any kind.

What caused the explosion no one knows. It was the defendants implication during the trial that the deceased fired a rifle shot against the door of the magazine. There is not the slightest evidence that the steel door was penetrated by a rifle shot. The lock was so applied that the key did not go entirely through the door.

The issue of the deceased shooting at the magazine was submitted to the jury and the jury found against the defendant on it.

An explosion did occur from unknown causes with such force that the powder magazine, made of ten inch concrete reinforced walls, was demolished and left rubble. Three people, including the son of the plaintiffs, were killed. Houses in the vicinity were damaged.

We approve and adopt, as certainly true, the trial court's conclusion, . . . that whether or not the existence of the powder magazine, under the circumstances shown by this record, was a nuisance, was a question for the jury.

The judgment is affirmed."

There the case ended.

I still wonder who decided to store hundreds of thousands of blasting caps in that powder house and why they never surrounded it with fencing. They could have put up a few signs warning of the danger, but they didn't.

We'll never know, just like we'll never know exactly how that .22 bullet entered the magazine and which of the boys pulled the trigger.

Life is full of unsolved mysteries.

# Lem Thomas Webb — Hubert Dale Prather — Leeman Bryan Webb

Lead Belt News; The hole blown in Paul Black's office by a huge chunk of concrete from the powderhouse.

Lead Belt News photo of a chunk of concrete from the powderhouse explosion. It ended up inside Paul Black's office.

Lead Belt News; The boy's bodies before being removed from the site of the explosion.

The Sad End of James Layton

Grandpa Province was a quiet man. Although I'm reticent to describe him as taciturn, I admit he was far from talkative. For one thing, he worked in the lead mines as a driller which negatively effected his hearing. His job was dangerous and constantly required his complete attention. There was generally no one else nearby to talk to anyway.

At work, he would climb the trapeze, drill holes, tamp in dynamite, light the fuses, and run like hell.

At home, it was a rare occasion when Grandma asked his opinion, so he was infrequent in offering it.

If I asked him a question, his response would be as frugal as one can imagine.

Thinking of Grandpa, I'm reminded of Calvin Coolidge, the 30th President of the United States. At a White House dinner, a woman remarked to the President, "I made a bet with a friend that I couldn't get you to say two words." Coolidge responded, "You lose."

That's the way Grandpa usually was. He would have been a lackluster interview on a talk show. *Yes* and *No* answers hardly constitute an intriguing conversation.

But, once in a while, if the stars were just right in the heavens and if I could catch him in just the right mood, I could sometimes get him to tell me stories. And, the stories he would tell me were well worth the wait; always interesting, entertaining, and often provocative. One day he told me a doozy.

It all started when the old man had some business in the County Court House in Farmington, Missouri and he took me with him. I was always bugging him to take me with him everywhere he went.

While he was inside the courthouse having some notary and photostat work done, I stayed outside in the car. He was taking longer than I expected so I exited the car and strolled around the courthouse, looking at the building. I've always liked old buildings. I especially like investigating old, derelict buildings and sneaking into the places where I'm not supposed to go. My daughter is the same way.

As I walked to the southwest corner of the street, across from the Ben Franklin store, I noticed a large concrete block buried in the ground. It had nothing written on it except for a large "X" which I thought was rather curious. Returning to the car, I got in, and sat there wondering what in the heck it all meant.

When the old man finally came out, I asked him about it. He said he wasn't sure, but he "thought" it might be where a hanging took place a long time ago, but he didn't know much more about it. He always said that when he didn't want to talk about something.

Well, that certainly got my attention. It was the first time I had ever heard of any sort of capital punishment in St. Francois County. Despite its morbidity, the whole idea peaked my curiosity. Fifteen year old boys are like that.

I began asking all my friends if they knew anything about it. No one in my circle of friends had any idea what I was talking about. When I asked my school teachers about it, they gave me an exasperated look, shrugged, and told me to find better things to do.

Then, I experienced an epiphany. That little light people talk about flickered on inside my inquiring young mind.

The Public Library!

Heck, the library had books about anything and everything. I was certain they'd have some record of a hanging on the grounds of the County Courthouse.

The next Saturday afternoon, I walked up the hill from my Grandparents house on Theodore Street, across Federal Hill past Conway Motors, down the hill on Main Street, across the Railroad tracks, through Schramm's Corner, and up the hill to the library on the corner of Science Street and High Street. The building was directly across from the High School grounds and Dunn's small store. It was a tiring walk, but I was positive it would be worth the effort.

Entering the library, I found the librarian, and asked her if she had any history books about St. Francois County. I explained what I was looking for and I could tell she was less than pleased with me and my request.

"Isn't that rather unwholesome for someone your age?" she demanded.

"No, ma'am, I'm just interested in local history," I said in defense. I made an attempt to look as studious as possible. Perhaps she'll think I'm writing a history book, I thought.

"Well, I say it's ghoulish," she sniffed, "But, we do have a book containing that subject matter. It's a reference volume so you can't take it out of the library."

"That's okay," I said, "I can read it here."

"Yes, it will be okay," she commanded, "and, yes, you will read it here."

She retrieved the book with the unwholesome subject matter but before handing it to me she said, "You can read it right there," pointing to a small desk next to her neat, methodically organized desk.

"Be careful with it," she admonished me, "It's an old book and you must treat it with respect. I'll be watching to make sure you don't damage it. And if you have a pencil with you, I'll take it until you're finished. I don't want you vandalizing the book with any unseemly scribbles."

I said, "Yes, ma'am. I don't have a pencil and I will be very careful."

As she handed the book to me, she said, "You know, if you continue to read this sort of material, it will rot your brain, young man."

I said, "Yes, ma'am. Nobody wants a rotten

brain."

I accepted the book, sat down at the small desk, and began to thumb through it. I had a feeling I might be pushing my luck if I asked for any help in finding what I was looking for.

I read the Table of Contents, which was no help. It dealt in generalities.

I turned to the back of the book to search the index.

I was looking for the word "hanging" under "H" but because I was reading the entire entry, I saw the words "Hardin hanging" near the top of the column.

I carefully followed the dot leaders across the page to the indexed page number. Under my breath, I said, "Holy cow." There were *two* page numbers; the second number was in *italics*. I knew enough about indexes to know that meant there was a *picture* on that page. It took a great deal of self-control to keep from going directly to the picture.

I went to the text page to see what it would tell me. Here's a summary of what I found:

The Hardin Hanging
January 23, 1880
by J. Tom Miles
The Farmington Press, May 1, 1936

The public hanging of Charles H. Hardin, on the southwest corner of the County Courthouse in Farmington, has been the only legal hanging in St. Francois County since its organization more than 100 years ago.

The execution was of such interest that spectators from as far away as Ripley, Bollinger, and Pemiscot counties were in attendance. By noon, on Friday, January 23, 1880, between 4,000 and 5,000 persons were gathered to witness the gruesome event.

Speculation had run high as to whether Hardin would make a public confession to the crime for which he had been sentenced to pay the supreme penalty. At 1 o'clock, he was taken from the County Jail and carried by wagon to the scaffolds, which had been arranged by Messers. Lang and Brothers.

With him rode his attorney (Jasper M. Burk), reporters from several daily newspapers, Major Thornbug (from Bollinger County) who had been summoned by Sheriff McMullin to adjust the ropes, and Reverend D.H. Parker, Hardin's spiritual advisor.

At the scaffold, Hardin slowly climbed the steps. He was dressed in a plaid business suit, a spotless shirt front, and a cravat. He knelt down to pray with Reverend Parker, then got up to talk to the crowd.

A portion of his last utterances were, "My sentence is a hard one, but it is just. I have nothing to say against the judge or the jury, or against Mr. Carter. He is a perfect gentleman. I think some of the witnesses didn't do me justice. But, I forgive them all. The people have treated me kindly and a good deal better than I had any reason to expect."

The large crowd was not disappointed that Hardin didn't make a public confession, but instead gave a religious oration, telling others not to follow in his footsteps.

At the trapdoor, he said, "Farewell vain world. This is the way Jesus supports a man in my condition."

Five physicians were on hand to pronounce Hardin's death. It was discovered that he had come to his death not as a result of a broken neck, but as a result of strangulation.

The Globe Democrat (a St. Louis newspaper) reported the idea that it was a cruelly managed affair. This had no foundation for the victim suffered little. His remains were placed in the County Graveyard. The scaffold was returned to Messers. Lang and Brothers, where it remained for some time, after which it was taken apart.

The location of Hardin's crime was a camping site on Indian Creek, near the village of Haggai, situated three miles southeast of Iron Mountain.

In October, 1879. Robert Ferguson was traveling from his home in Kansas to Illinois, where relatives of his lived. His transportation was a wagon drawn by a team of horses. With him was his five-year-old son, John.

Several days before the murder, Mr. Ferguson was joined by Charles H. Hardin, who was also driving a span of horses, borrowed from a Mrs. Best, in Sedalia, Missouri.

On Sunday, October 26th, 1879, they camped at the fatal site. Mr. Ferguson had $350 with him when he left Kansas. Mr. Hardin wanted this money and this is the way he managed to get it:

After the evening meal, Mr. Ferguson was sitting on a stool before the campfire. Hardin picked up a stick, as if to stir the fire. He turned suddenly and struck Ferguson. Several such licks crushed his skull, and he soon died. Two days later, the partially submerged body was discovered by the children of some campers.

In the meantime, Hardin had taken the plunder, one wagon, the four horses, and the small boy. He escaped by train to Columbus, Kentucky, but was brought back to Farmington to stand trial.

A letter found on Ferguson's body led to his identity and because a card was also found showing him to be an *Oddfellow* in Franklin County, Illinois, he was buried in Farmington's Oddfellow's cemetery.

On Tuesday, December 2nd, 1879, Charles H. Hardin was brought before Judge Nicholson for trial. The hearing was conducted in the old Lang building, since the courthouse was condemned at this time.

Attorneys for the state were Prosecuting Attorney Francis M. Carter, the Hon. J.F. Bush, and Merrill Pipkin. Lawyers for the defendant were Messers. Jasper M. Burks, and J.W. Bennick.

Testimony was completed in a few days and it took the jury only 20 minutes to arrive at a guilty verdict. The execution of Charles Hardin was the only legal hanging in this county.

On June 14th, 1843, James Layton was hanged from a beam just south of the County Jail by an angry mob who stormed the jail, and removed Layton by force.

I sat there looking at the final paragraph of the report. I re-read it. Then I re-read it again. "Geez," I thought, "If Hardin was the only guy hanged *legally*, who the heck was this Layton guy?"

I risked bothering the librarian by asking, "Excuse, me, ma'am, but have you ever heard of somebody named James Layton?"

"No, I haven't," she said, "Are you finished with that book?"

"No, ma'am," I said, "Not quite."

"Just be careful with it," she said.

Instead of answering her, I flipped the page over to see the seven decades old photograph of the Hardin hanging. I studied it intently, as I do with all photographs. As I sit here writing this, I've just realized the photograph is now 135 years old.

I agree with the old saying, "A picture is worth a thousand words." I don't just look at pictures, I study them. I look at everybody and everything in the picture - especially the background - and then I try to think of how many stories could be told from that one picture.

I couldn't help but notice there were men, women, and children in the picture. They lined the streets, crowded onto the courthouse lawn, and were hanging out of the windows of the courthouse. When they ran out of space, they climbed onto the roof of the courthouse. They climbed the trees surrounding the courthouse square. And what for? To get the best viewpoint for watching a man die. There were thousands of them present for that single purpose.

It was apparent that I wasn't the only one interested in this gruesome piece of St. Francois county history. The difference is that I don't believe I would have attended the hanging. I was viewing the spectacle from the comfortable distance of almost seventy-five years, seeing it as an historical occurrence. But, that seventy-five year span also gave me the moral distance in addition to the distance of time. Had I been alive back then, I can't honestly say if I would have been there to witness the killing of a man.

I must have been very deep in thought, because the librarian was tapping me on the shoulder with her pencil and saying, "I'm talking to you, are you awake? Are you through with that book?"

I pulled myself forward to the present and said, "Yes, ma'am. I'm finished. Thank you for your help."

I handed the book to her, got up, and left the library. During the walk back home, my mind was full of unanswered questions and chilling images. I realized the one thing that I had read, but had not fully registered in my brain.

" . . . the only *legal* hanging in St. Francois County . . . "

That kept running through my head as I

slowly strolled down Theodore Street and into our front yard. I sat down on the porch swing and took a little rest before going inside.

Entering the front door, I looked around and realized it was very quiet. The television was off. There was no one in the living room. Grandma's chair was empty, which was a rarity.

I said, "I'm home. Is anybody here?"

I heard Grandpa back in the kitchen, "I'm back here fixin' some tea, you want some iced tea? Nice and fresh and cold!"

Grandpa loved his iced tea. He always made it from fresh tea leaves which he boiled. He refused to use, " . . . them new fangled tea bags."

He would boil a handful of tea leaves to make an exceptionally rich concentrate and then pour it over a large glass full of ice to make it cold. A couple of spoons of sugar and it was ready to savor.

I said, "Yes, sir, that sounds pretty good. I've just had a long walk. Where's Grandma?"

He said, "Woman's Club meeting at the *Blue Flame Room*. Gone 'til late this evening. Took your brother. Naomi picked 'em up half an hour ago. Took his accordion to entertain the ladies."

That brought a smile to my face. I said, "So it's just you and me?"

"Yep," he answered.

I still had thoughts running around in my head and I figured now would be as good a time as any to try to get Grandpa in a talkative mood. But, I had to play it *cool*.

As he handed me a large glass of iced tea, I

said, "I've been to the library."

"Oh, yeah?" he said.

I said, "Yes, sir. I was reading a really interesting story, but there's something I don't understand. It's supposed to be a true story."

I didn't want to say too much. I was hoping to get him interested enough to start a conversation.

"True story? What about?" he said.

Good, I thought, I got the nibble, now if I could just hook him.

"About a big concrete slab in the ground at the courthouse in Farmington," I offered.

"Oh, that," he said as he gave me a sly smile.

"Yes, sir. I went to the library to check it out and found a book with a story about it. It's supposed to be the only *legal* hanging to ever have taken place in St. Francois county," I said, "It was supposed to have taken place in 1880."

He took a big drink of his tea and said, "Yes, it did. Five years before I was born. Pap told me about it. He was there with a whole bunch of other folks. I think he told me about it to scare me from going into a life of crime."

"Geez," was all I could get out.

"From what Pap told me, something went wrong with the scaffold trap and the fella didn't drop just right. Instead of breaking his neck, like it was supposed to, he just twisted around until he strangled to death. Not a purty picture is it?" he asked.

"No, sir, it's not. Pretty rotten picture if you ask me," I said.

He gave me a serious look and said, "Well, purty rotten for him, I suppose, but then you gotta think about the fella he beat to death. That's purty rotten, too. I figure he got what was coming to him. If you don't want to be on the wrong end of a rope, you shouldn't go around beating people's heads in."

I just said, "Yes, sir, I mean, no, sir."

We sat for a couple of minutes drinking our tea. I made little faces in the moisture on the glass.

I said, "Good tea."

He said, "Yeah, it's one of the things I *can* do right, no matter what your Grandma says," and he laughed.

He pointed his large finger at me and said, "Don't you tell her I said, that, now,"

"No, sir, I won't. I've got secrets of my own," I said.

He said, "I can only imagine. Doesn't everybody?"

We sat there for another quiet minute and I finally said, "There's one thing I don't understand about the story I read, Grandpa."

"And what might that be," he asked.

"At the end of the story it said the Hardin hanging was the only *legal* hanging in the county. How many *illegal* hangings have there been? I've never heard of one," I said, "They never mention that stuff in school."

"There's only one as far as I know," said Grandpa, "and that was before my time, too. My Pap was only five when it happened, just like me. His Pap, my Grandpa, came home one day and told everybody about it."

I had to think about that for a minute. I said, "Hmmm, his Pap would be my Great-Great Grandpa? Boy, that's going back an awful long time."

I could almost see the wheels working in Grandpa's head as he thought about that and then he said, "Yeah, your Great-Great Grandpa. My Pap was born in 1838, and the lynching was in 1843 I think, so Pap would've been five years old. His Pap, who everybody called Grampa Joe, was born in 1810. He knew folks who fought in the American Revolution. He would have been seventy-five when I was born, if he had lived that long. I don't remember him."

"Five generations of us Provinces," said Grandpa, "We go way back. Missouri, Tennessee, North Carolina, Scotland, England, France, who knows what all."

"So what happened?" I asked.

"The lynching?" he asked.

"Yes, sir," I confirmed.

"Funny about something like that, ain't it? Folks like to talk about those sort of things. Grampa Joe told my Pap, my Pap told me, and now I'm tellin' you. What is it about folks wanting to know about bad things and bad people?" he asked.

I said, "My English teacher says it's called *The Human Condition*. She talked about it in class one day. We had to write a story about why people do the things they do. She said people are the only animals that think about thinking. She said that's what philosophy is; thinking about the meaning of life, reasons for being alive, and people having too much curiosity for their own good. She says that's why people cause so much trouble in the world. Sometimes I get together with the other guys in class and we talk about that stuff."

"Well," said Grandpa, "As far as I'm concerned all that philosophy stuff is a bunch of falderal. Nothing but gimcrack nonsense, if you ask me. I've never seen any animal that got drunk, or beat his wife and kids, or killed somebody for a few silver dollars. Some folks just plain ain't no good. I don't need any five dollar words to know there's a lot of good-for-nothing folks who ain't worth the powder it'd take to blow 'em up. Like Judge Roy Bean said, 'I've never seen a horse that needed to be stolen, but I've seen plenty of men who needed to be hanged.'"

Trying to sound grown up, I said, "Yes, sir, the world's full of 'em Grandpa."

"All I can tell you is what my Pap told me," he said.

I listened intently to the story he told me and I've tried to put it to paper as close as I can remember it:

First off, it didn't even happen here. It happened in Perry county, but we'll get to that.

During the night of June 17, in 1841, a fella named James Layton came home drunk, just like he always did. He was a useless, desolate, and worthless human being if ever there was one. He never provided for his family, but he still expected his wife to have supper ready whenever he got home. On the fatal night, he came home drunker than usual and when he found his wife had nothing on the table for him, he became enraged. She tried to explain, but he wouldn't listen.

He slapped her around and kicked her out of the house. Forced her outside, into the dark, freezing night. For good measure, he snatched up his little boy and threw him out the door, too. It mattered little to him that a fierce winter storm was raging outside.

Mary was her name. She was his second wife, the daughter of Richard Maddock and Elizabeth O'Connor. It was later discovered that at the time of her vicious murder, she was, in fact, with child.

Layton's first wife died, leaving him with a young son. It was reported that the boy was also a victim and he suffered greatly from the evil disposition of his drunken father.

Having been thusly thrust into the winter storm, Mary and her nine-year-old stepson attempted to make their way through the darkness to a neighbor's house.

Layton wasn't finished, though. After the consumption of even more corruptive drink, he became more angry. He decided to pursue them and punish them further.

The two frail fugitives made their way to a spot where earlier that day some laborers had been clearing brush. The workers had tried to burn the green cuttings of the days work and there remained some embers glowing in the darkness. Mary and her stepson attempted to warm themselves over those ebbing fragments.

It was while they were crouching over the charred coals that the drink maddened demon burst upon them, from the thick woods, with disastrous results.

Layton took grasp of a heavy limb that had been burned to a point and struck the poor woman on her head, bringing her to her knees. Ignoring her plea for mercy, he continued to beat the helpless and unresisting victim until her life was extinct.

Then, with a brutality that even an ordinary savage would have eschewed in horror, Layton, with all his might, thrust the burned point of the club through her body, pinning the poor woman and her unborn child to the earth beneath them.

Realizing, through his drunken stupefaction, what he had done, he turned, and ran, fleeing the scene of this heinous, this hideous, crime.

He left his little boy at the scene of the appalling slaughter, the singular witness to the whole despicable affair. The small, frightened child left his dead stepmother in the night and made his way to the neighbor's house, thereupon relating the horrific, tragic story.

The next morning, at the earliest light, the neighbors assembled at the scene of the murder and they were justly shocked at what they saw.

Though at that time, the telegraph was

unknown and newspapers were few and far between, news of the evil crime spread quickly through Perry County, as well as adjoining counties.

In spite of a huge manhunt for the miscreant, it was a full year before James Layton was arrested. He was found hiding in Wayne County and was brought back to Perry County where he was put on trial with the charge of first degree murder.

His own son, the little nine-year-old boy, was put on the witness stand. In spite of his youth, the boy's courage and testimony was so clear and convincing, no amount of cross-examination by Layton's lawyers could confuse him nor refute his relating of the events of that night. The events were burned into his memory.

Upon the conclusion of the trial, the jury conferred for no more than ten minutes. They brought in a unanimous verdict of guilty and Layton was sentenced to be hanged by the neck until dead.

Interest in the case continued in the minds of the local citizenry. Once the sentence had been passed, everyone, it seemed, was looking forward to the brutal end of the cruel murderer. Everyone, that is, except the murderer's family.

Spurred on by Mr. Layton's parents, his lawyers appealed the conviction until it arrived at the door of Missouri's Supreme Court.

As often happens in the company of lawyers, the court determined that the trial should be set aside and the case was remanded for a new trial with a change of venue to St. Francois County.

Mr. Layton's rights, they said, must not be violated. He must receive a fair trial.

In May, 1843, the Layton Case came up for trial a second time. As before, Layton's son was the only witness called. And, as before, his father was convicted and sentenced to death. The day for atonement was June 17.

Owing to the frightful features of the murder and the over-long legal delays that followed its perpetration by the murderer, people were demanding justice, and rightly so.

Layton had been convicted twice and sentenced to death twice. People felt it was time for him to meet the gallows.

By 10 o'clock on the morning of June 17, more than 300 people gathered in the public square in the small village of Farmington, Missouri. Many of them had traveled thirty miles or more to witness the execution.

The prisoner was housed in a jail of two-story log structure. The first story was constructed with triple walls for security.

Access to this "dungeon," as it was referred to by locals, was by a trap-door through which the jailer descended by means of a movable ladder. Once the ladder was drawn up, the trap-door was shut and securely locked.

A few minutes after 11 o'clock, the sheriff, with considerable effort, pushed his way through the dense mass of humanity to the foot of the stairway leading to the jail.

As he ascended the stairs, people noticed that

he had a piece of paper in his hand. They assumed this to be the *death warrant* to be read just prior to the execution. They were wrong.

As the sheriff reached the top of the stairs, he paused. There was a breathless silence throughout the crowd. He announced to the crowd that the paper he held in his hand was received only a few minutes ago. It was a directive from the Governor of the State of Missouri.

The sheriff, shifting from one foot to the other, visibly nervous, held up the paper for all to see. He explained that it was, in fact, a *Ten Day Stay Of Execution*. The effect of his words seemed to spread through the crowd like a bolt of electricity, creating an almost tangible, palpable sense of anger.

At first, there was a murmur of dissatisfaction from them, but as they talked, the murmur became a roar of indignation. It was at that moment the *crowd* evolved into a *mob*.

They had come to see a hanging and, "By Godfrey," they wanted a hanging.

"If the sheriff won't hang the murderer," said someone in the mob, "then we will!"

A few of the more conservative members of the group tried to calm situation, but they were out-voiced the majority.

Someone yelled for a "vote" to be taken. All in favor of the hanging would stand on one side of the courthouse lawn and those against would stand on the other side. Very few individuals moved to the "against" side of the courthouse lawn.

A rush was made on the jail. Using heavy iron bars and sledgehammers, the door was beaten down. The trapdoor was pried up and a half-dozen lynchers descended into the "dungeon." They tied the prisoner's hands behind his back, tied a rope around his neck, and carried the trembling wretch up the ladder to the second floor, and out onto the platform at the head of the stairs.

Horses were unhitched from an open buggy, which was backed to the foot of the stairs. The victim was placed into the buggy and it was moved to a spot under a gallows-tree which was improvised for the horrid occasion.

The apparent leader of the mob held his hands up to quiet the crowd. He asked the culprit if he would like to say anything, but Layton was too frightened to speak. He was quaking in terror.

The rope around his neck was thrown over the beam and secured to the buggy, which was immediately pulled from under the murdering reprobate. The body swung back and forth for several moments while he kicked wildly in the air. Within a few minutes, however, the body became deathly still.

The evil, brutal murder of Mary Layton was avenged.

The mob calmed down and became a crowd once more. Having completed the grisly task, the people quickly dispersed from the scene of the lynching. When it was safe, the sheriff cut down the body, which was buried as quickly as possible.

Most of the area's citizens held the conviction that the actions of the mob were as much the fault of Missouri's Governor, Thomas Reynolds, as it was the individuals making up the mob.

The murderer had been given two separate trials in two separate counties. He had been sentenced to death twice. And, yet, the governor repudiated the legal outcome of both trials, attempting to delay the proscribed penalty with his stay of execution. At least, that's the way the citizens saw it.

Layton's lawyers had been grasping at straws, looking for loopholes in the law, and as lawyers are wont to do, they did everything in their power to prohibit the law from expending justice. They instructed Layton's father to write a sad, tear-stained, letter to the governor begging for the stay of execution until the lawyer's "points of law" could be assessed a second time by the Missouri Supreme Court.

When the governor acquiesced to the lawyers request, the citizens became fearful that Layton would be allowed to slip through the legal system and justice would be mocked. The people would have none of it.

Following the lynching, Layton's father wrote another heart-wrenching letter to Governor Reynolds, thanking him for his help. In this letter he insinuated that the mob consisted of people from Perry County and that the lynching was instigated by Richard Maddock, Mary

Layton's father.

James Layton's son (James Layton, Jr.) was taken in to the home of his grandparents, Richard and Elizabeth (O'connor) Maddock.

John Layton and his wife Monica (Layton's parents) eventually left Missouri and moved to Texas.

And that was the end of the story.

By the time Grandpa ended the story, we had each finished another large glass of tea and I needed to pee. When I came back, I said, "Boy, that's quite a story, Grandpa. Is it all really true? Would people really act like that?"

He said, "Well, all I can tell you is that's the way my Pa told it to me. It was a long time ago and who knows if it's all true. I'm sure some parts of it were embellished over the years, but for the most part, I reckon it's true. As for the lawyers, I know they're all as crooked as a dog's hind leg."

He continued, "Well, It's my turn now. You clean up everything while I take a pee. Your Grandma and Harold will probably be back in a couple of hours and we don't want them seeing a big mess in the kitchen."

I started washing up. When Grandpa came back I said, "You know Grandpa, people still do things like James Layton did. Why do they act that way?"

Grandpa chuckled and said, "Maybe its like your teacher told you. What's the fancy name she calls it?"

I said, "*The Human Condition.* That's what

she said it is."

He said, "Yeah, well, there's lots of humans and lots of conditions. Folks never really change, though, do they?"

I said, "That's pretty sad. I hope I never turn out that way."

Putting his hand on my shoulder, he said, "I think you'll be okay. We started you off in the right direction, anyway."

I said, "Yes, sir, I guess so. Hey! How about I find something to watch on television?"

He said, "I'll go get situated and you take care of the TV."

I finished drying and putting away the dishes and went to the living room to watch TV with Grandpa.

The longer I sat there, spending time with Grandpa, the less I thought of the crimes of Mr. Layton.

Life goes on.

Above: St. Francois County Courthouse as I remember it in the 1950s.

Below: The "X" marks the southwest corner of the Courthouse grounds where Charles H. Hardin was hanged on January 23, 1880.

Above: An early photo of Flat River's Public Library, where I researched the Hardin hanging.

Below: Public executions have always been popular. Notice the nice folks in the trees and on the courthouse roof.

A Day On The Diamond Drills

I think I was about ten or eleven when the old man used his union seniority at the St. Joe Lead Company to bump into a job as a Diamond Drill Operator.

It was a Saturday evening and for once, the whole family was sitting at the supper table. That would be Grandpa, Grandma, Harold, me, and the old man, who usually had somewhere else to be on a Saturday night. He was a busy man.

In addition to his full time job in the lead mines, he was also the Mayor of Flat River. His mayoral duties required a lot from him and he was in demand for all sorts of official, and unofficial, political functions. Even a small town like Flat River, Missouri required a lot of work.

We were finishing off a big pot of Grandpa's homemade chili and we were listening to the old man in between his big gulps of buttermilk, which he loved. He was telling us how much he was looking forward to being able to be out in the fresh air for a change.

I asked him, "A diamond drill? I didn't know you drilled for diamonds in the lead mines."

Grandpa said, "I wish there were diamonds down there. I could have paid this house off years ago."

The old man shook his head and said, "No, we don't drill for diamonds. The tips of the drills we use are encrusted with industrial grade diamonds. That makes them bore through the rock quicker and easier. Holes are bored into the ground and when we pull the hollow pipes out, they have rock cores in them that we mark so the assayer knows where the lead deposits are."

"Boy, that sounds pretty cool," I said. "I sure would like to see how that works."

"Daddy doesn't have time to drag you along to work with him," said Harold, almost reading my mind.

"I haven't even started the job yet," added the old man.

"I'd still like to see how it all works," I said.

I was pleasantly surprised when the old man pushed away his plate, emptied his glass of buttermilk, and said, "You know, once I get situated on the job, I might be able to do that. We're always way the heck out in the boondocks somewhere and there's never anyone around but the drill operators. I guess no one would know even if you were there or not."

Grandpa said, "I think it's a good idea. The boy could learn a lot. What do you think?" he asked, turning his toward Grandma.

Grandma hesitated and then said, "If he promised to stay away from the machinery and keep his hands off things, it might be okay. I don't want him coming home minus any fingers."

"Or maybe his big fat nose," said my beloved brother Harold.

"We'll have none of that kind of talk at the supper table," admonished Grandma, pointing her finger at him.

That didn't stop Harold from making an ugly face at me.

"I'll tell you what," said the old man. "School's gonna be out soon and you won't be moving out to the farm for a couple of weeks after that. I'll see if I can't get all fixed up on the job and then take you with me one day. How's that sound?"

I said, "That sounds pretty darn good."

And with that, everybody left the table.

The old man went to his room to change clothes and get ready for his usual Saturday night festivities.

Grandma went into the living room and sat in her chair. Harold followed her and turned on the television.

Grandpa and I removed the dishes from the table and we washed them together. Grandpa never minded cleaning up and I never minded helping him. I asked him to tell me a story about when he was a kid.

He said, "We never were kids. As soon as we could walk, Pap had us working the farm. We all had chores to do and if we didn't do them, we would get a real strapping."

Then he told me about his grandfather and how some Indians stole his fish after he had been fishing all day. He bent down and said in a low voice, "Did you know there was a lynching once right here in St. Francois county?"

Wide-eyed, I said, "Really? Holy Cow. Tell me about it."

He smiled and said, "Maybe one day. Not today, but, maybe one day. I don't want your Grandma thinking I'm filling your head with all kinds of unpleasant ideas. You know how she gets."

He left it at that and we went out to the living room to watch some television.

Grandma was already ensconced in her big over-stuffed chair and Harold was sitting on the couch behind her. Grandpa sat down in his big over-stuffed chair on the other side of the room next to the fireplace.

I moved my chair to the center of the room and settled myself for the evening's entertainment. "Settling in" was far from a permanent situation, though. Grandma kept the newspaper on the little table next to her and she would study the evening lineup. After a show was over, she would inquire as to who wanted to watch what and we all offered our input even though we usually watched what Grandma and Harold wanted to watch.

When the big decision was made, I would get up, go to the television, change the dial to the proper channel, make sure all the settings were correct, and then return to my chair. In those early days of broadcasting, televisions were analog devices which had vertical and horizontal synchronization settings. Additionally, the brightness and contrast could be adjusted to obtain the best possible picture. It was a far cry from the digital TVs of today.

Receiving a watchable picture also depended on the size of the roof antenna and if it was pointed in the correct direction to pick up broadcast signals. The earliest antennas only picked up VHF channels. Newer, fancier antennas had additional reception elements for bringing in UHF broadcasts.

Believe it or not, there were a few rich people in Flat River who had television antennas with rotary motors on them. The antenna could be rotated for the best reception simply by turning a knob on a box near the television. Go figure.

Of course we never had such a frivolous convenience. It was easier for me to sit on my knees in front of the television and adjust the picture until Grandma yelled, "That's it! Don't touch it!" In most cases I didn't have to alter the settings again unless we changed channels.

Of course, if you lived in a big city like St. Louis (like my aunt Theresa did) all you needed was a set of "rabbit ears" on your TV set. There was no need for superfluous fancy gadgetry like a roof antenna.

We would usually start the evening's entertainment with *You Asked For It*. Grandma never cared much for Art Linkletter so we never watched *People Are Funny*.

After that, it was *The Jack Benny Show* followed by *Private Secretary*, starring Ann Sothern. It was silly stuff, but I liked Ann Sothern.

When ABC started showing reruns of Jack Benny, we switched to NBC and watched Wally Cox as *Mr. Peepers*. They were reruns, but we hadn't seen them so it made no difference to us.

Next on the Saturday evening entertainment agenda was *Toast of The Town*, later renamed *The Ed Sullivan Show*. Grandpa and I enjoyed the show because the majority of the acts were old vaudevillians.

I have fond memories of the Nicholas Brothers; the Wiere Brothers; Ben Blue; Lowe, Hite, and Stanley; soft shoe dancers; Johnny Puleo and the Harmonica Rascals; "Professor" Backwards; "Professor" Irwin Corey; Olsen and Johnson; tightrope walkers; chimpanzee acts; dog acts; jugglers; plate spinners; Apache dancers; and the whole gamut of vaudevillians who were glad to have the opportunity to perform their acts once again.

One act I never understood was a woman dressed as a snake who slithered all over the stage. But, that was vaudeville, it was on television, and it was free.

We would usually end the evening with *What's My Line* with moderator John Charles Daly or perhaps *Break The Bank* with the always affable Bud Collier. Another of Grandma's favorites was the ever inspiring *Loretta Young Show*, which was always heartwarming and pleasant. Oh, some trivia about Bud Collier: he was the first actor to portray Superman on the radio.

Although excellent dramatic anthologies were

broadcast during this "Golden Age of Television," we only occasionally watched shows like *General Electric Theater, Philco Playhouse, Westinghouse Theater, Studio One,* or *Playhouse 90.* It was Grandma's often-voiced-opinion that many of the shows should never be telecast into people's homes. They were unsavory to say the least.

Dramatic endeavors such as *The Days of Wine and Roses*, and *What Makes Sammy Run* were provocative and unwholesome for general public consumption. Stories about alcoholics and the immorality of Hollywood were not good for young minds. She was visibly incensed upon discovering that Sammy Glick (*What Makes Sammy Run)* actually said, "Damn," not once, not twice, but three times! It's no wonder the world is going to Hades.

We rarely watched anything on the DuMont Network. Grandma said they were second rate and "low brow" shows. She held a specific dislike was for *The Honeymooners*. While that show is considered a "classic" by many people today, she held the belief that Ralph Cramden was nothing more than a loud-mouthed, offensive, blustering bully. She was adamant when she asked the question, "How could anyone think someone like him is funny?" She preferred the "big three" networks; ABC, CBS, and NBC.

The only exception to Grandma's television tyranny was on Friday nights and that was because of what Grandpa called "The Friday Night Fights." The proper name for the show was *The Gillette Cavalcade of Sports* and every friday night, a boxing match was broadcast all the way from Madison Square Garden in New York City.

Grandpa never missed the boxing matches. I never cared for them, but I watched them because he did. I can vaguely hear the faint refrain of a tune somewhere in my mind . . . a band playing the *Look Sharp, Be Sharp March*. I can almost see a dim cartoon commercial showing a guy getting a "really close shave." The announcer is speaking; "Good evening, ladies and gentlemen, it's the *Boxing Event of the Week* brought to you by the *Gillette Safety Razor Company*."

It was a rare fight when somebody actually won by a knockout or even a TKO. It was mostly a couple of plodding palookas shuffling around the ring throwing an occasional punch in the hopes it might do some damage to his opponent. The winners of most of the fights were chosen by points awarded by two ringside judges and the referee.

I hadn't paid a lot of attention the shows that particular Saturday evening, though. I had been thinking about the old man's "sort of" promise to take me to work with him one day if things worked out. I thought about it every day for the next few weeks, too. I never bothered him about it, though, because I didn't want to jinx the whole thing.

The weeks went by, school let out, and Grandma began planning our move to the farm for the summer.

Then, like bolt out of the blue, it happened.

The old man came home from work on a Thursday afternoon and as he walked in the house, he said, "Well, do you think you can be up and ready by 6:00 a.m. Tomorrow?"

Like a deer in a car's headlights, I was stunned for a few seconds, but I finally spit out, "Heck, yeah! If you want, I can be ready at 5:00 a.m."

He laughed and said, "Oh, no, 6:00 a.m. will be just fine. There's no need to be nuts about it."

He had a paper bag in his hand and as he headed toward the kitchen, he nodded his head indicating I should follow him.

We got to the refrigerator, which I still called the "ice box," and he took a few things out of the paper bag as he showed them to me. He said, "I stopped by Honbeck's on the way home and picked up some extra lunch meat, a fresh loaf of Pan Dandy bread, and a couple of big cans of Vienna Sausages. You think these'll be enough for our lunch?"

I said, "I think that'll be swell. What're we drinking?"

"Royal Crown for me and I thought you'd like a Nehi Chocolate," he said, showing them to me.

"Boy, I really like chocolate soda. Thank you!" I said with a big grin.

He put everything in the refrigerator and said, "I've got somewhere to be in a few minutes, but I'll be home in plenty of time to make sure you get to bed and get some sleep."

He left and I couldn't stop thinking about the unbridled possibilities that lay ahead.

I know we watched something on television that night, but I couldn't tell you what. I had bigger things on my mind.

The morning arrived and at 6:00 a.m. we were in the car; lunches packed, drinks in the small cooler, and things to do.

We drove for almost an hour, down a few lonely backroads, finally pulling up to a wide spot off a gravel road in a heavily wooded area. I think we were somewhere between Flat River and Saint Genevieve. I had been lost soon after we left the house.

The old man set the brake, put the car in low, and turned off the engine. He pointed to a bunch of heavy machinery a few yards away and said, "See all that equipment over there? That was dropped off yesterday by the survey crew. This whole area is about ten acres and we have to drill all over those ten acres. See that big stake in the ground over there? That's where we drill first. Each stake has a number on it and when we pull the core sample out of the drill we put them into trays with the same number written on them. That way the geologists know exactly where the ore samples come from."

I was trying to take it all in and with a furrowed brow I said, "Yes, sir, I understand."

Getting out of the car, I noticed a small Caterpillar next to what I knew must be the diamond drill. Next to the drill was a small shack on big wooden skids and next to that was a large water tank on wheels.

Just as we were walking over to the shack, I

heard an old, thoroughly beaten up Ford pickup truck crunching down the grave road at a slow, deliberate pace. It was apparent the driver was in no hurry at all. We watched him turn in to the clearing and park next to the old man's dark maroon 1954 Ford sedan. The pickup truck reminded me of the Joad family's truck in *The Grapes of Wrath*.

A tall, lanky weed of a man stepped out of the truck and sauntered toward us. I got the impression that he never did anything quickly. As the old man later said, "He has two speeds, slow and stop."

As the man moseyed up to us the old man pointed to me, put his hand on my shoulder, and said, "This is my youngest boy, Mike. He's going to be with us today so he can learn all about diamond drill prospecting."

He turned to me and said, "This is my drilling partner . . . ," and I can't remember if he said his name was Festus, Eustus, Rufus, or Cletus, but it was something like that. I'll just call him Festus.

Anyway, Festus nodded his head, put his hand out, and said, "Hells Bells, young fella, you're the spittin' image o' yer old man. I hope I don't git all confused like and start callin' you Herman!" He laughed like it was the funniest thing anyone ever said.

I looked at the old man, who just raised his eyebrows, and I said, "Yes, sir."

Having gotten the civilities out of the way, the old man said, "Well, Festus, we better get this operation set up and running. We need at least one set of core samples ready for the assayers today."

"Yeah, I reckon so," agreed Festus.

The old man climbed into the Caterpillar seat, started it up, and drove it to the front of the drill. Festus hooked up a set of chains from the drill to the Caterpillar and the old man pulled it to a spot next to the stake in the ground. Next, they dragged the shack next to the drill so they could step directly onto the drill platform from the shack.

While the old man began to check the drill and its engine, Festus opened the shack and started getting things in order. Entering the shack and pointing to the left side with his long, skinny thumb, he said, "This here's my side. T'other side's your pa's. But I don't care if you wanna sit on my side. It don't matter none to me."

I said, "Thank you. I'll see how it goes for now."

"Suit yerself, young feller," he said.

I noticed the old man's side of the shack had nothing on the wall but Festus' side had all sorts of things hanging from nails pounded all over his wall; caps, gloves, belts, and handkerchiefs. There were even a couple of old "girlie" calendars that were far from current. On the bench below, there was a small shelf which had fallen off the wall when the shack was jostled by the latest move.

After hanging and readjusting everything that

had fallen, and reinstalling his small shelf, I noticed he had a huge stash of chewing tobacco. There was *Beechnut Rough Cut, Skoal Fine Cut, Red Man Plugs, Mail Pouch Twists,* a variety of *Skoal Snuff,* plus other brands I had never heard of. He could have opened a chewing tobacco store.

I was no stranger to chewing tobacco. My Uncle Herman (Aunt Theresa's husband) was a user of the stuff. He wasn't allowed to smoke in the house so he opted for chewing his tobacco in the basement.

During a visit to Uncle Herman's and Aunt Theresa's one year, he took me along to his Masonic hall for a meeting with his fellow Masons. On the way there, I noticed he was driving slower than usual and a few moments later, I understood why. He reached down and from under his car seat he pulled out a large coffee can. He spit a huge load of tobacco juice into it and then continued his discourse on the Masonic Brotherhood.

Before thinking, I said to Festus, "Gee, that's a lot of tobacco."

He looked at me and said, "Yeah, I cain't stand them there cigars and cigarettes. They stink to high heaven and lotsa folks hate the smoke. My wife don't like it none neither. I jist never picked up the habit. Chewin' ain't no problem, though. It don't bother nobody."

He glanced at the old man and almost whispered, "Didja ever try chewin' any 'a this stuff?"

I said, "No, sir, I haven't."

He grinned, bent his head toward me, and said, "Ya know, if'n ya wanna, I wouldn't give a lick if'n ya snuck a little taste of it . . . ya know, jist to give it a try . . . an' I wouldn't say nuthin' to your pa if'n ya wanted."

"Yes, sir. Thank you. Maybe some other time," I said.

Giving me a big wink, like we were partners in crime or some such thing, he turned around and stepped out of the shack.

He finally got serious and started helping the old man get the drilling rig up and running.

As I watched, I became very much impressed (as much as a nine year old kid can be) by the old man. It was quite an operation and it took a lot of knowledge and ability to run everything involved. He had to be able to operate a Caterpillar, run the drill, run the generator that supplied power to it, and he had to know how to fix anything that might break down. It was hard, dirty work and for all his trouble, he was paid about $25.00 a week, which was darn good money for a lead miner.

When we had arrived at the drilling site, the old man gave me a pamphlet to read. It was a tri-fold containing a rudimentary history of *The St. Joseph Lead Company.* There were even a couple of paragraphs about diamond drills in it.

It started with the comment that St. Joe was the largest producer of lead and zinc in the United States. I already knew that.

The company was founded in New York City

in 1864 by Lyman Gilbert, John Wylie, Edmund Wade, Wilmot Williams, James Dunham and James Hathaway.

J. Wyman Jones, the company's first president, acquired a mine in Bonne Terre, Missouri originally owned by a man named LeGrave. It took some time for people to stop calling it *LeGrave's Mine*. It was this mining operation that was raided by Confederate Army General Sterling Price.

Jones and his newly hired Mining Manager, Charles B. Parsons, introduced the use of "diamond drilling" techniques to their business and it turned out to be one of the best decisions Mr. Jones made. It gave the company exact information as to where large deposits of galena (lead ore) rested deep within the earth.

Parsons was actually "Doctor" Charles B. Parsons. He was a dentist who had been commissioned as a Captain in the Union Army but was forced to resign his commission due to poor health. He was an intelligent, creative man with numerous abilities and astute business acumen. He gave up the practice of dentistry to go to work for St. Joe. He devised a number of mechanized operations that made mining operations easier and he made a lot of money for the company.

Parsons read an article in a magazine regarding a new invention called a "diamond drill". It was a device that could cut deep into rock and using a hollow bit and hollow pipes, it could bring up samples of the rock through which it had drilled.

After being educated about the new drilling rig by Dr. Parsons, Mr. Jones presented a report to the Board of Directors requesting money to purchase a drilling rig for the company. He was more than surprised when he received an extremely odd and unexpected response.

Their objection to the expense was based on the idea that " . . . more ore had already been discovered than could possibly be processed in several years . . ." using the current methods of mining operations.

Jones wrote a report which he gave to each board member and he went through his proposal in detail, patiently explaining that this was a good thing for the company and not a liability. He told them this was an excellent opportunity for expansion and that an expansion of operations would make more money for the company. Reading this, I found it curious that such an endeavor would have to be explained to men who were supposed to be businessmen.

After the meeting, the Board of Directors approved the requisite funds and on March 5, 1869, a diamond drill rig arrived in Missouri.

The initial drilling was started close to the Hathaway incline and the drill reached the depth of ninety feet but samples displayed only a few specks of ore. The rig was moved about 50 feet to the south-east and the crew drilled to a depth of 75 feet, but once again the samples provided no better results.

Upon receiving reports of these results, the Board of Directors told Jones to stop drilling because it was a waste of money. Jones, however, was adamant and he instructed Parsons to continue drilling in secret and he (Jones) would personally pay for the operations if necessary.

With these instructions, Parsons returned the same spot where the drill had only gone 75 feet into the ground. His plan was to see how how deep the drill could go. At the depth of 150 feet, core samples proved there was an immense body of galena below. This may be where the old diamond driller's adage came from to, "Go deep or go home."

The use of diamond drills was the first step toward the modernization of St. Joe's operations. In the years to follow diamond drills located huge areas of rich ore - almost pure - all over the Lead Belt.

Further reading of the pamphlet informed me that St. Joe, like all large corporations, interpreted laws to their advantage if possible. The state of Missouri had enacted statutes in 1890 and 1891 prohibiting mining companies from owning more land than was *absolutely* necessary for their mining operations.

To circumvent this obstacle, St. Joe created a "holding company" named *The Bonne Terre Farming and Cattle Company* in 1891. By turning over all mining operations to the "farming and cattle company" St. Joe was able to ignore the law and continue as though nothing had happened. This is how lawyers earn their money.

On August 4, 1900, the Hoffman tract was purchased and a shaft sunk in 1901. A small army of carpenters were brought in to build worker's houses and a company store was established. On October 12, 1901, a Post Office was established using the name of Owl Creek, which was the name of a nearby stream. The citizens apparently disliked the name of Owl Creek, so they petitioned the Post Office Department to rename the town. The petition was approved in 1902 and the town of Leadwood was born.

By 1923, St. Joe had over 250 miles of underground railroads running under the towns of Flat River, Leadwood, Desloge, Rivermines, and Elvins. It was like a small city down in the mines.

During the Depression of the 1930s, St. Joe suffered along with the rest of the country. But, instead of halting operations, as many companies did, the company reduced operations to one week per month. The company also provided community gardens for its employees to raise food for their families. During the winter months the company allowed employees to cut wood on company land for heating and cooking. To remain solvent, St. Joe borrowed $10,000,000 and managed to stockpile thousands of tons of lead concentrates.

I often like to remind people that contrary to popular belief, President Roosevelt did not get the country out of the depression. Most of his programs were dismal failures. It was World War II that saved the United States. War is very good business and Roosevelt couldn't wait for the chance to get the country involved in the war.

By the end of 1945, St. Joe had more than 3,000 employees working full time on three shifts seven days a week. It was during the war years that the employees unionized. The 1940s and 1950s were boom years for the St. Joe and its employees.

When I finished reading the pamphlet, I turned my attention to the work being done on the rig's platform. I watched everything they did. I was fascinated at how it all worked.

After setting up the rig and starting the generator that ran the whole thing, the old man and Festus started by screwing a large diamond drill bit onto the first drill pipe and started it boring its way into the ground.

As the drill spun round and round the bit continued to bore ever deeper into the earth's crust. Water from a big tanker was continually poured into the hole to keep it lubricated.

When the pipe had bored its way into the ground and had about 4 feet showing, the rig was put in "neutral" and another pipe was pulled off the rack, pulled up by a rope until it was vertical and the threads were mated to the pipe in the ground. When the pipe was tight, the rig was taken out of neutral and the drill continued grinding its way toward the center of the earth. It was a simple process, but to a little kid, it was an amazing spectacle of mechanization.

Pipe after pipe after pipe was driven down into the earth for about three hours.

Finally, when the required depth had been reached, the whole process was reversed. Pipe after pipe after pipe came back out of the hole.

Each pipe was unthreaded and thrown back on the rack where it came from. The difference was that as each pipe was separated from the pipe beneath it, the core samples had to be removed.

The pipes were pounded with a bowling pin to loosen core samples so they would slide out. The samples were placed in a large wooden tray with numbers on it indicating rig placement and depth of sample.

The old man was taking a break and sitting with me in the shack. As I watched Festus pounding the hell out of the pipe with his bowling pin, I asked, "Why is he using a bowling pin? Why doesn't he use a rubber mallet?"

"Festus likes his bowling pin," said the old man. "He found a box of them by a trash can outside a bowling alley one night after he and his wife finished a league game. They love to bowl. You should ask him about it." And then he laughed.

I wasn't sure if he was being serious or what, but I figured it couldn't hurt to find out.

By the time all the pipes had been brought up and cleaned out, it was time for lunch.

The old man asked Festus if he wanted the

first lunch and Festus said, "Naw, I ain't gonna eat for a little while more. You'n yer kid go ahead and have yer vittles."

The old man said, "All right. We're going to eat in the car."

Festus said, "Hell, yeah. It'll sure be quieter than here," and he laughed. Festus liked to laugh.

We sat in the car and ate our sandwiches, which were delicious. They were very possibly the best sandwiches I ever ate in the history of sandwich eating. Next we opened our tins of *Vienna Sausages*.

The old man held out his tin, just like it was a glass, and said, "Here's to a good day at work. I'm glad you're here to help out."

I held out my tin and we "clinked" our *Vienna Sausage* tins together. I said, "You betcha, Pop!"

The old man said, "Go deep, or go home!"

I repeated, "Go deep, or go home!"

We drank off the flavored water in the tins and laughed. Then we slowly ate the scrumptious little sausages. I was having the time of my life.

The old man pulled the *Nehi* Chocolate Soda out of the little cooler, popped the cap off it, and handed it to me. I wiped the ice water off the outside of the bottle and wiped my hands on my pants.

He pulled his Royal Crown soda out, popped the cap off, and did the same.

He drank his in two gulps and let out a belch.

Copying him, I did the same. I'll admit that

my belch was a bit forced, though. Chocolate soda had no fizz.

We sat for a few more minutes before he said, "I guess we better get back so Festus can have his lunch."

I said, "Sounds fair to me."

We got out of the car and ambled back to the rig. The old man was holding my tiny hand inside his catcher's-mitt-sized hand as we walked.

The old man took over the drill and Festus went to his beat up old truck and ate his lunch. I seem to remember him talking about having a huge slab of headcheese on homemade bread. His wife loved to bake and her specialty was bread.

As Festus returned to the rig, I remembered what the old man said and I asked him, "How come you use that bowling pin?"

Festus looked at me funny and I wondered if I had offended him. He said, "That there's a damn good question, little man. I ain't never had nobody ever ask me before."

He seemed to think really hard for a few seconds while he organized his thoughts. He went over to the rig, picked up the bowling pin, and brought it back into the shack. He handed it to me and said, "Here ya are. Grab yer mitts on that there and give it a feel. Fer some reason, it just fits the hand like it was made fer it. It's got that there little head where ya kin grab on it easy like an' ya kin control it, ya know? It's made of good, hard wood and it's got a little bounce on it when you hit the pipe. There ain't nuthin' else I've found what kin smack the hell outta the pipe like bowling pin does without stingin' my hand. Now, you go on ahead and tell me that don't feel good . . . even in yer little hand."

I have to admit, it did have a good, solid, balanced feel. I liked it. "It does feel good," I admitted.

"Hell, I use 'em fer everthing what needs to be whacked. Got a whole box of 'em," he said.

I handed it back and said, "Thanks, Festus, that all makes sense."

I think he liked me calling him by his name. He smiled and said, "Hell, yeah." Then he spit a huge glob of used up tobacco on the ground, reached for the *Beechnut* pouch, took out a small wad and stuck it in his mouth between the cheek and the jaw. He nodded his head and said, "I love this stuff."

He started out of the shack, looked at me and said, "Yer a good kid. And yer old man's a good guy. I'm glad he brung ya with him today."

I said, "Thanks, Festus. You're okay, too."

He laughed and said, "Hell, yeah!"

Things slowed down a bit after that. The early morning, the long day, the lunch, and the constant din of the drill was getting to me and I was trying to stay awake.

They were able to pull one more set of core samples out of the ground and into the trays before having to shut down for the day. Every chance he had, the old man would come into the shack and sit with me and tell me about how everything worked. We even talked a little bit about how much we still missed Mama.

On the way home, I must have dozed off. I remember the old man gently nudging me and saying, "We're home, kiddo. You've had a big day. You should sleep pretty well tonight."

I said, "Yes, sir, but it was a really good day. Thanks for taking me with you."

"Yes, it was a good day," said the old man, "I'm glad you came along."

Before we went into the house, I gave him a big, long hug and he hugged me back.

It was one of my best days **ever**.

The older I get, the more I miss the old man.

The type of television set a rich family would have owned during the 1950s.

Prospecting for lead ore with a Diamond Drill Rig. "The old man" ran one just like this in the early 1950s.

Above: Diamond Drill Bits.

Below: Core samples out of the bits.

The Great Rebellion of '62

We all do things we're not proud of. Sometimes our actions are out of spite and sometimes we do things impetuously without considering the repercussions. Even a tiny pebble thrown in a lake can make ripples.

As much as I dislike having to admit it, I was part of something that caused a lot of trouble, hurt a lot of people's feelings, and I'm very sorry I was involved. It was one of life's great lessons for me.

I could offer the excuse that I was young and didn't realize what I was doing, but that doesn't change anything. As someone once said, "You can't un-ring a bell." I was seventeen years old and enough of an "adult" to be held accountable for what I did. I don't know if any of the others involved had misgivings later on, but I certainly did. I learned an important lesson on thinking things through before making stupid decisions.

It happened during my senior hear at Flat River High School. A lot of the kids in our class were simply tired of school and especially tired of the senior year. The nearer we got to graduation, the more we wanted it over and done with.

Our music teacher was Annie Louise

Huggins. She was almost five feet tall and that was with her shoes on. She was a short, chubby gal who had been teaching high school music classes for decades. She was what one might call a "fixture" at the school.

I think that may have been part of the problem, but I can't really blame Miss Huggins for all of it. She had been at the high school for so long, she had a certain way of doing things, and she became upset if things didn't go the way she expected.

On the other side of the fence were the boys in the senior music classes. By the time we were half-way through the school year, we realized that we held a certain amount of power if we all stood together, acting as a group with a single purpose. We understood what "pack mentality" meant.

In our music classes, we were part of the *Glee Club*, the *Madrigal Club*, and four of us made up the *Senior Quartet*. That would be Larry Getz, Frank Dunn, Bill Stallings, and me. You wouldn't think a musical group could cause a lot of trouble, would you? Well, you'd be wrong about that.

One of the problems was that Miss Huggins refused to listen to us when we told her we really didn't like some of the songs she selected for us to sing. We thought them were downright silly.

One song in particular we hated was a "sea shanty" called *All For Me Grog*. Here's the chorus from the song:

And it's all for me grog, me jolly, jolly grog
All for me beer and tobacco
I spent all me tin on the lassies drinking gin
Across the western ocean I must wander

See what I mean?

This stupendously ridiculous song was the catalyst that lit the fuse of *The Rebellion of '62*.

We had been working on the song for a week and no one liked it except Miss Huggins. She kept telling us it was supposed to teach certain musical conventions. We kept telling here it was just plain stupid.

The *Senior Madrigal Club* and the *Senior Quartet* were scheduled to perform at a number of community gatherings. We had already performed at the opening of the new Flat River Post Office in 1961 and at a couple of school assembly programs. We were now preparing to perform at a city function which was highly publicized and which would draw a large crowd in the Field House where important functions were held. It was the biggest performance of the school year and a lot of people would be there.

We had been working on our repertoire and Miss Huggins was growing nervous about the performance. Being a bit high-strung, she complained about everything we did and nothing we did pleased her. She was nit-picking every note that came out of us and we were tired of having someone pick our nits.

I was on the wrong end of one of her tirades one day when she stopped pounding her piano, pointed at me, and said, "Stop sliding your notes! Be precise!"

Trying to make a joke out of it, I said, "I'm singing like Bing Crosby would do it." And I smiled.

She, however, was not smiling. Her face hardened and she said, "Well, you're *not* Bing Crosby, and you *never* will be. You're a high school student and you have to do this the way I tell you to do it."

That comment certainly removed the smile from my face. The thought flickered through my mind, "Oh, yeah? Well, I'll show you."

Unfortunately, I wasn't the only person in the room to be the recipient of her flaring temper. She had said a few caustic things to some of the girls and one of them was almost in tears.

Things continued like this for a few more minutes and then she said something to one of my friends, Larry Getz. After her sniping remark, he said, "Well, maybe you don't even need me if I'm as bad as you say I am."

That's when it happened.

She said, "If you don't like the songs I pick you don't have to stay here and sing them. You're free to leave any time you want; no one's stopping you."

I think the clock on the wall may have actually stopped for a few seconds. The room became quiet, we students looked each other, and then back at Miss Huggins.

Larry said, "Do you really mean that?"

Miss Huggins went further. She slowly

surveyed the class and said, "No one has to stay here if they don't like it. Anyone who wants to can leave right now."

I think she realized too late what she was saying even as the words came out of her mouth. She looked a little bit scared.

I was watching Larry as she voiced her ultimatum. He stood up and looked at me. I could almost read his mind as he gave me a look that said, "Are you with me?" I knew exactly what he was going to do and I nodded slightly to him. I stood up.

He and I looked at every other boy in the class and slowly, one by one, every one of them stood up: Frank Dunn, Bryan Brand, Alan Lundmark, and Jim Tucker. The lone exception was Bill Stallings. It was no surprise when he stayed behind with the rest of the girls.

Larry and I walked to the center of the room and out the door. All the others followed us. When we were all in the hallway, someone mumbled, "Jesus Christ, man, now what do we do?"

"I don't know if we should have done that," said another voice.

"We're probably all going to be in a lot of trouble," commented another.

"If we all stick together, there's nothing they can do to all of us," Larry said.

I said, "This class is an elective. It won't even matter on your grades. They're going to have to cancel all the performances for the rest of the year."

With that, we all left the Field House and walked up the street to the High School building. I'm not sure what all the others did, but I went to my locker and got my books for the next class.

The next day none of the guys attended Miss Huggins' class. We didn't know it at the time, but in today's vernacular, people would say we were "boycotting" her.

The day after was the same. And on it went for a full week. No one was talking about it openly. Walking down the hallway, I could tell that other students were pointing at me, just as they were with the other guys who were "on strike."

The situation came to a head on the next Monday morning. A couple of the other guys parents heard about what happened and they contacted Gayle Simmons, the principal of the high school. Miss Huggins had, of course, informed him of our recent "rebellious" activity.

The Monday in question started as Mondays in school always start, but during the first class of the day, every "striker" was given a note to be read in private. Each note said we were all "requested" to meet with Principal Simmons at noon that day for a "discussion" of certain school issues.

We all showed up at the appointed time, were ushered into the Principal's office where a couple of rows of chairs had been set up, and we were "invited" to make ourselves comfortable. We were told the Principal would be there in a few minutes.

While sitting there, waiting for Principal Simmons to arrive, one of the guys said, "I don't understand this note. Why are they "requesting" us to be here. Why didn't they just tell us to be here?"

I said, "That's a euphemism."

He said, "What the heck is a *you-pho-whatz-im*?"

I said, "It's a nice way to say something that would sound bad if you said it outright."

Larry piped up, "Yeah, like when a doctor says this might hurt a little but you know you're in for it big time."

One of the other guys said, "Oh, man. I don't like the sound of that."

Larry said, "Just hang tough and we'll see what happens."

I said, "Yeah, we haven't committed any criminal offenses. We're just standing up for our principles." I'm not sure if I was trying to make myself believe we had done the right thing, but I was a bit uncomfortable. I didn't show it, though.

Another guy said, "Man, oh man, I don't like this. Maybe we shouldn't have left like we did."

Just then, the well appointed door opened and Principal Simmons entered. He looked at all of us and smiled. He walked to his desk, sat down, and said, "Thank you for coming, gentlemen. I understand there's a problem between you young men and Miss Huggins. May I speak to all of you honestly and frankly?"

We all looked at one another and wondered who should answer. We hadn't thought about having a spokesman for the *Madrigal Seven.*

Larry took the lead, saying, "Yes, sir, I think we're all open to a discussion."

I said, "A discussion would be a good thing, along with an explanation of *why* we did what we did."

Principal Simmons adjusted his seat and said, "I've already had a talk with Miss Huggins. She feels badly about what happened and how she reacted. She asked me if I would offer an apology for her. You know, all she really wants is for the Madrigal Club and the Senior Quartet to perform to the best of their abilities. One of the problems is that we've already scheduled performances with the *Lions Club* and the *Rotary Club* and those performances have been widely advertised. People are expecting the school to be represented there."

We sat there while Principal Simmons seemed to make some notes on a pad of paper in front of him. He continued, "I think it's important that you all be aware of something. I'm not at liberty to give any specific details, but I can say that Miss Huggins has been under a bit of personal stress lately. All she wants right now is to go back to the way things were before this unfortunate situation developed. Now, what is it that you young men want?"

From our lack of immediate response, it was apparent that we really didn't *know* what we wanted.

I realized that I was impressed with the way Principal Simmons was handling things. He was disciplined, positive, firm, and polite. He was treating us as adults and showing us respect that I'm not so sure we deserved. I gained a great deal of admiration for him that day.

Since no one else was talking, I said, "I think we should be allowed to choose some of the songs we sing. Some of the ones we're told to sing are pure nonsense. I'm really tired of *Moon of Manakoora* and *All For Me Grog*. Who sings sea shanties about grog these days?"

Jimmy began to hum the tune to *Moon of Manakoora* in my ear.

I turned around and said, "Knock it off."

Principal Simmons said, "Mr. Tucker, we're not here to perform right now."

Larry said, "How about us singing a couple of songs Miss Huggins wants and a couple of songs we want? As long as one of then isn't *All For Me Grog*?"

Principal Simmons chuckled, "*All For Me Grog*. I don't think I like that one either. I've never quaffed a grog in me life."

Everyone in the room visibly relaxed after he said that, especially since he said it in a pirate's voice. No one expected him to be funny.

He continued, "Larry, that sounds like an excellent proposition. I'll speak with Miss Huggins and inform her of our discussion. I'm certain she will agree to it."

I couldn't help but notice that all of a sudden we were all on a first name basis. I guessed we weren't going to be keelhauled after all.

After a slight pause, he said, "There is one additional thing I'd like to ask of you young men, if you don't mind."

He became serious, looked at each and every one of us in turn and said, "I would be greatly appreciative, and accept it as a personal favor, if all of you would *please* be nice to Miss Huggins. Perhaps we can simply go back to the way it was before this happened and not even mention it again. Is that possible?"

Larry said, "Yes, sir, I can do that."

I said, "Yes, sir, I can, too."

All the other guys chimed in and agreed to the arrangement.

Principal Simmons continued, "Then we will move forward from this moment. I'm expecting you gentlemen to honor your commitments and perform at the scheduled appearances for the rest of the school year. Miss Huggins will be expecting you at the next class meeting."

We all said, "Yes, sir."

He stood up, said, "Well, I guess we're all done here, then. I'd like to thank you for helping to fix this problem. And remember, gentlemen . . . if you have *any* questions or problems, please come to me first so we can talk before anyone does something rash."

With that, he shook hands with every guy as we filed out of the room.

As promised, we attended the next class meeting and every class after that until the end of school. We practiced, we sang our songs as scheduled, and I like to think we all felt much better for having completed the school year in a positive manner.

The last time I saw Miss Huggins was after I spent three years in Germany in the army. I had returned to Flat River and matriculated at Flat River Junior College.

I encountered Miss Huggins in the hallway one afternoon. She seemed to be quite a bit older than I remembered her, but she was as nice as pie to me and I returned the sentiment.

I discovered that her schedule allowed her to leave school at the same time I finished my last class. Since she lived just a couple of blocks from the college, I offered to give her a ride on those days I was attending classes. She was no longer able to drive.

I only attended the college for a single semester before leaving Missouri and moving to California. On the last day at the college, I dropped her off at her little house and said goodbye.

She said, "You're a very nice young man, Mike. Thank you for the ride."

I replied, "Thank you, Miss Huggins. It's my pleasure."

Above: The Senior Male Quartet; L-to-R; Mike Province, Bill Stallings, Frank Dunn, and Larry Getz.

Below: The Senior Madrigal Club before *The Great Rebellion of '62*. After the walkout, the only singers left were Bill Stallings and the rest of the girls.

Dr. Gayle Simmons, High School Principal and arbitrator of the *Great Rebellion of '62*.

Miss Annie Louise Huggins; she could be tougher than a two-bit steak.

Getting The Lead Out

Well, here I am in the middle of volume three of *A Little Kid From Flat River* and I've suddenly been attacked by an epiphany. I've realized how remiss I've been about mentioning both Flat River's part in the history of lead mining and how the lead mines worked.

It occurred to me that there are people being born in "Park Hills," Missouri who will have no idea that Flat River even existed, let alone have any education about how mining works. I shall, indeed, have to rectify this lamentable omission.

I was prompted to this realization when my daughter, Michelle, posed some questions after proof-reading my *Carbide Lamp* chapter. I've completely neglected her education about how a bunch of rocks can be turned into pure lead.

I've previously explained (perhaps too much so) that the "powers that be" have destroyed my Grade School, Junior High School, High School, and Junior College.

I've also complained about the wholly unnecessary destruction of the Chat Dumps that were part and parcel of my childhood as well as an impressive, visual reminder of the lead industry itself.

I've even let my feelings be known about how

the town of Flat River, itself, was destroyed by the loss of the mining industry and compounded by the merging of Flat River, Elvins, Esther, and the village of Rivermines.

Thomas Wolfe was spot on when he wrote the immortal line, "You can never go home again."

With all that in mind, I've decided to offer a brief summation, a short history lesson as it were, about how my old man, my grandpa, and other relatives, earned a living in the lead mines.

I'm certain the day will come when someone living in Park Hills will say in all innocence, "Flat River? Lead mining? Chat dump? I have no idea what you're talking about. That's just crazy talk."

If nothing else, I will have kept a modicum of history alive pertaining to an area once known as *The Lead Belt* and referred to as, "The largest lead producing area in the world." I have a nagging feeling that if I don't do this, the 250-year history of lead mining in southeast Missouri may be lost forever.

Of course, I may be wrong about that, but I don't want to take that chance. Losing our history and heritage would be a terrible shame. I wonder if they even bother to teach any of this to today's "Park Hills" school students.

Pay close attention, kiddies, there may be a pop quiz later.

The earliest report of the discovery of lead in what would become southeast Missouri mentions a man by the name of Penicaut, who was both French and a member of the LaSueur

Exploration Party. Penicaut supposedly found lead ore (Galena) erupting from the ground somewhere along the Meramec River.

This discovery prompted the King of France, Louis XIV (aka the *Sun King* or *Le Roi Soleil*), to grant "Crozat Patents" in 1712, providing special privileges for the development of mining interests in *his* Louisiana Territory.

What gave the *Sun King* the right to all this property has never been adequately explained to me.

In 1717, John Law, the French Comptroller General of Finances, obtained those "royal patents" for his "Mississippi Company" and mining preparations were haphazardly initiated. He was also the one who came up with the idea of creating the "plantation economy" throughout the Lower Louisiana Territory and importing African slaves into the Louisiana Territory. I remember my Grandpa talking about their descendants from time to time, always referring to them as "those Black-French."

Just to cover all the bases, I should mention that the Louisiana Territory encompassed all or part of 14 current U.S. States and two Canadian Provinces (Alberta and Saskatchewan). The 14 states are Arkansas, Missouri, Iowa, Oklahoma, Kansas, Nebraska, parts of Minnesota west of the Mississippi, most of North Dakota, almost all of South Dakota, northeastern New Mexico, portions of Montana, Wyoming, and Colorado east of the Continental Divide, and Louisiana west of the Mississippi River, including the city of New Orleans.

That's a lot of territory for a Frenchman to claim as personal property. I guess being a King really is a good thing, at least until the people revolt and chop your head off with a guillotine.

Times change, though, and all of this real estate was eventually put on the market. I can only imagine the size of the *For Sale* sign required for so much acreage.

Napoleon Bonaparte had installed himself as the First Consul of the new French Government in 1799, following a *coup d'etat,* and his incessant wars were straining his budget.

Needing the money, Napoleon sold "his" property to Thomas Jefferson in 1803, a year before he crowned himself *Emperor of France.*

Jefferson picked up the 828,800 square miles of land for a mere $11,250,000 plus the cancellation of $18,000,000 worth of U.S. debts to the French. In today's dollars, that would be $219,000,000, which is chump change for the Federal Government these days.

I'm not that good at math, but I think it works out to about 42-cents an acre. I sure would like to get in on a deal like that.

As odd as it may sound, Thomas Jefferson later wrote a personal letter to a friend in which he admitted the only reason he purchased the Louisiana Territory was to acquire the city of New Orleans. Jefferson considered New Orleans to be of paramount strategic importance to the up and coming United States government.

The French certainly left their mark on

certain parts of Missouri. As late as 1890, five years after my Grandpa's birth, the town of Florissant, which is now a St. Louis suburb, had a predominantly French speaking population.

The French influence remains in the state of Louisiana, too. Even to this day, the *Napoleonic Code* is the basis for the laws there and Louisiana Counties are called "parishes."

Between 1719 and 1825, mining in "Missouri" was spotty to say the least. In 1769 the settlement at *Mine-La-Motte* was attacked and destroyed by Chickasaw Indians, causing the abandonment of mining operations until 1780.

More discoveries were made at *Mine-A-Layne* about 16 miles southeast of Potosi, and in 1797 the first authentic discovery in "St. Francois County" was recorded in the location of *Mine-A-Maneto*, on Big River.

In 1801 *Mine-A-Joe*, later called *Bogy Mine*, was also started on Big River.

In 1806 heavy mining productions started in St. Francois County at a place called Hazel Run, about five miles northeast of Bonne Terre. It was reported that 500 tons were produced here during the first year.

In 1824 Joseph Schultz discovered the *Valle Mines*, seven miles north of Bonne Terre, and in 1825 *Bisch's Mine*, near *Valle Mine*, was opened for business.

During this early period of mining activity, lead ore was entirely galena, obtained from shallow surface digging. Miners seldom dug more than ten feet in depth. Even this surface level ore consisted of eighty per cent pure lead.

The St. Joseph Lead Company was organized in 1864 when it purchased the *La Grave Mines* at Bonne Terre. The following year full operations began on the property after the completion of a mining, milling, and smelting plant.

In 1869, "modern" lead mining operations began when St. Joe introduced Diamond Drill explorations and immediately discovered immense ore deposits dispersed at a depth of 120 feet.

"Surface mining" methods came to an abrupt end and operations headed underground. Milling methods were also revolutionized and gradually ideas and concepts of circumspect mining plants came into being.

In 1880, St. Joe began building railroads to adequately move the huge tonnage being brought up from the mines.

In 1890 the town of Flat River came into existence and the growth of the industry was nothing short of phenomenal.

By 1923, St. Joe had expanded exponentially, buying out the Doe Run Lead Company, the Federal Lead Company, the Desloge Consolidated Lead Company, and the National Lead Company along with its St. Louis Smelting and Refining Works.

Although the industry suffered along with the rest of the nation during the Great Depression, the Second World War revitalized the economy and St. Joe was going great guns into the 1960s.

By the 1970s, production costs, environmental issues, and government regulations all helped to run St. Joe out of business in Missouri's Lead Belt. The company closed operations in Flat River in 1972.

So much for a cursory examination of the history of lead mining in southeast Missouri. The question remains, "How does the ore become lead?"

What follows is a synopsis of what is required to turn ore into lead.

It all starts with Diamond Drills equipped with hollow "diamond set" bits that chew through whatever substance they encounter. The cores brought to the surface in the hollow pipes reveal the exact composition of the ground and whether or not lead deposits are present.

After deposits are located by the drilling explorations, a shaft is driven into the center of the surveyed area and "drifting" is radiated from the main shaft in whatever direction the vein of ore demands.

Some mines are as shallow as four hundred feet while others reach a depth of seven or eight hundred feet. Deep mines may have as many as four or five levels where ore is produced. In deep mines, huge pillars are left on top of each other at planned intervals to support the roof and prevent cave-ins.

In the old days, ore was loaded by hand and brought to the hoists on narrow-gauge railway cars drawn by mules. That's how things were done when Grandpa began working in the mines.

Today, however, miniature railway systems comprise hundreds of miles of tracks that are in daily operation. Locomotives travel back and forth throughout the various drifts leading to active headings. Cars go out empty and come back full, each car carrying at least a ton of ore which is taken to bins that are elevated to the surface of the hoisting shaft.

Underground operations are made up of four basic actions; breaking, loading, haulage, and hoisting.

Breaking is accomplished by drillers; men equipped with air-driven drills (similar to jack hammers) that drill holes into the face of the rock. The idea is to bring down as much rock as possible with the least number of holes and least amount of dynamite. To accomplish this, miners work in two shifts; one for Breaking and one for Loading and Haulage.

When Grandpa started working in the mines, drilling was a two-man job done with hand tools. A hole was started by pounding a short cross-tipped chisel with a small sledge hammer. When the hole was deep enough, the short chisel was replaced by a much longer one. One man would hold the chisel in place while the other man laid into it with a large sledge hammer. After each strike of the chisel, it would be given a quarter turn to break the rock as quickly as possible. Using this method, a couple of miners could drill a quite a few holes in a relatively short time. It was hard, tiring work and the men switched places on the sledge hammer often. I learned how to do this when I helped Grandpa drill holes into the concrete wall going down into his basement so we could install a handrail.

After drilling the holes, miners charge them with dynamite and prepare them for firing. After the drilling shifts have left all of the mine's levels, the drilling foremen fire their holes at a safe distance, carefully counting each shot in their particular headings to make sure they all fire.

If all the shots fire properly, the drilling shifts leave the mines and no work is done in that drift until the arrival of the next shift, which gives the air time to circulate and remove the dynamite fumes from the workings. Dynamite fumes can give a miner a violent headache and intense nausea so its imperative that the air be given a chance to be cleaned.

Loading is the first operation following freshly fired shots, but no one is allowed in the heading until the roof (called "the back" by miners) is examined by "Roofmen." It's their job to locate any "loose" (hanging masses of rock) that might break loose while men are working.

Falling loose has probably killed more miners than any other type of mining accident. The Roofman must pry down anything he deems to be a danger to a miner. No work of any kind is allowed in the drift until the Roofman says it's okay to continue and no one is allowed to counter-order a Roofman's judgment. When he gives the go-ahead, then and only then, will loaders be allowed in the heading.

Grandpa Province was a Roofman. He would swing on a rope held by a steel bar driven into the back. A backup man would assist him, moving him up and down to get at the loose to bring it down. It's one of the most dangerous jobs in the mines and he was good at it. He also worked the "trapeze" which was a series of scaffoldings hanging from the back.

In Grandpa's day, loading of ore was done by hand, but today, machine loaders are used which are capable of loading as many as two hundred cars in a single shift. If a boulder is found that's too large to be handled, or if it's so massive that it blocks access to the heading, holes are drilled into it, a small dynamite charge is set, and it's blown apart.

Haulage is accomplished by large "motors" which are driven to and from headings at regular intervals, distributing empty cars and retrieving loaded cars. Each motor is assigned to a specific territory and is responsible solely for that area. Trains of cars are picked up by "transfer motors" after regular motors have accumulated loaded cars. On occasions when steep grades are encountered, "double-headed motors" are used to pull the train of cars from the heading to the "hoisting shaft" for removal to the surface. Motors, purposely built to be low and squatty, weigh between six and ten tons. Even though they are built for power in the handling of rock tonnage, they are capable of high speeds.

Hoisting shafts are normally located in close proximity to the crushing unit of the milling operations, if at all possible. Two types of hoists are used in the mines; one is a "man controlled" hoist operated by a hoisting engineer on the surface; the other is an "automatic electric" hoist.

The man controlled hoist is operated according to a series of signals from bells and air whistles.

The automatic electric hoist, which is more efficient with very heavy tonnage, is an amazing innovation of engineering brilliance and has to be seen to be appreciated.

In both cases, however, the ore is hoisted to the surface in a specially constructed "bin cage."

Milling is what happens after the broken ore has been brought to the surface by the hoist. At this point, the "miner's work" is done.

The ore is then ready for the final operation called "milling" which begins with the rock "crushers" and ends with the lead being extracted from the rock. As with the mining operations, "milling" is divided into several unique operations; crushing, concentrating, and flotation.

Crushing is accomplished by "gyrafory" crushers. These monster-sized, conical-shaped machines are open at the top allowing for ore to be dropped into them directly from mining operations.

As the ore is dumped in, the huge, conical

apparatus rotates to grind and crush it into small chunks. Ore is fed in using the "pan conveyor" which has specially constructed buckets to carry the rock.

Crushed ore ranges in size between 1-1/2-inches to 2-inches and is carried to storage bins located in the mill. From these bins, the ore passes over a 10-mm screen which effectively removes all smaller sizes of rock. Larger pieces are passed through the "roll section" where they are further reduced in size until they can drop through the 10-mm screen.

At this point, things become more "technical" in nature.

Ore passes through a series of "tabling operations" which includes moving the ore over jigs, vibrating tables, through de-sliming processes, and re-grinding machinery, all of which is accomplished in water.

The lead, being so much heavier than the rock from whence it came, is easily separated and by the time the process is completed, what is left is "lead concentrate" consisting of about 80-percent lead.

The concentrate is loaded into waiting cars while the waste rock, called "trailings" or "chat" is taken away from the plant and added to existing "chat dumps."

The used water, still containing a percentage of lead particles is carried off to the "flotation" section for further treatment.

Flotation extracts lead from the water and slime that was used in the milling process. The water is pumped into settling tanks where "solids" are allowed to settle and the product is picked up once again, mixed with water in a 1-to-4 ratio, and run through "agitation" machinery.

Creosote is added to the mixture at this point and the thickened mass is violently agitated and passed once more into settling tanks. From here it is drawn off and pumped to "dryers," thence loaded and shipped to the smelting plant.

The flotation process is imperative because the concentrate normally averages about fifty-percent lead, making it much too valuable to discard.

Smelting is done at the end of milling operations. The lead is sent to the smelter where it is roasted and furnace-blasted to refine the material to 99-percent purity.

The end product - molten lead - is cast into 100 pound ingots which are sold to manufacturers who require lead in their products; e.g. building construction, lead-acid batteries, bullets and shot, weights, solders, pewters, fusible alloys, and radiation shields.

And, there you have it; the mining, the milling, and the smelting processes, as I remember them, right up to 1972 when mining operations ceased in Flat River. This is how Lead Belt miners "got the lead out."

I've already explained the job of Roofman but I want to re-emphasize the importance of that job. What follows is an obituary of Charles LaChance, one of many miners who were killed by falling loose. The coroner in the case was my Uncle Eulean, the youngest of my Grandparents five children.

Charles Franklin LaChance of Esther was instantly killed last Friday morning, January 22, 1937, in an accident at No 11 shaft where he was employed by St Joe Lead Company. He was 44 years old.

The accident happened at 8:00 a.m. LaChance and three fellow workmen, Henry Dennis, James Jordan, and George Gilman were removing loose back when a section gave way and caught LaChance beneath it, crushing him to death.

Coroner Eulean Province conducted an inquest at seven o'clock Friday evening, the verdict being that the deceased came to his death as a result of being crushed by falling rock.

Funeral services were conducted Sunday at 2:00 pm at the Church Of God in Esther and burial was in the Woodlawn Cemetery, in charge of the service was Hood's Mortuary.

Charles Franklin LaChance was born in Mine La Motte, MO., September 12, 1892, the son of Mr & Mrs James Andrew LaChance who now reside at Knob Lick. On December 24, 1914 he was united in marriage to Catherine Isabella Rodgers, who survives him. The couple had no children. Besides his widow and parents, he leaves mourning his death a sister, Mrs Millie Hollinger of Knob Lick, a brother; Joe LaChance of St. Louis, and a great many friends and relatives.

For more than 250 years men worked the mines in southeast Missouri, including my old man, my uncles, my two grandfathers, and the fathers, uncles, and grand-fathers of all my schoolmates from the 1940s to the 1960s. It's all gone now, even the chat dumps.

I could write a book about the lead mines, I suppose, but there are two reasons why I don't. First, no one would read it; second, no one really cares any more.

Above: Drilling in the drift.

Below: Drilling in the back (roof).

Above: Tamping dynamite and setting fuses.

Below: Lighting dynamite fuses.

Above: Clearing loose from a
newly blasted drift heading.

Below: Continual clearing of loose
from old headings and back.

Above: Loading ore into a single car.

Below: Loading ore into a train of cars.

Above: A transfer motor moving a loaded train to the hoist shaft.

Below: Hoist buckets bringing ore from the shaft to the surface for milling.

Above: Surface hoist structure
bringing ore to the milling area.

Below: Dumping hoisted ore onto a transfer
belt on the way to the rock crusher.

Above: Ore is dumped into the crusher
as the enormous cylinder rotates
and breaks it into small pieces.

Below: Water used during the initial
separation process is repeatedly settled
and agitated to extract remaining lead.

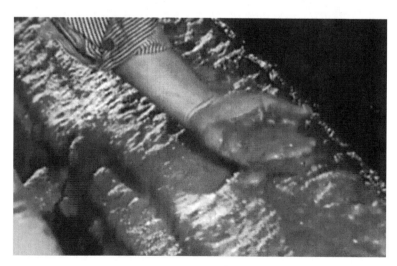

Above: At the smelter, milled lead is furnace blasted, refining it to 99-percent purity.

Below: From the smelter, the molten lead is cast into 100 pound ingots ready to sell.

Above: 100 pound ingots from the smelter.
This stack weighs 3,500 pounds.

Below: The process; ore on the left, tailings (chat) on the right. Lead concentrate in the middle and the finished ingot in front.

Above: A Steam powered Diamond Drill in use when Grandpa Province started working in the lead mines.

Below: A large hunk of pure lead. I have a few of these that the old man gave me.

My father, Herman H. Province, Sr., (aka The Old Man) hard at work at the controls of a transfer motor in the St. Joe Lead Mines.

How I Got An "A" In Algebra

During my twelve year sentence in the educational system, my memory is void of the slightest enjoyment of numbers, arithmetic, mathematics, algebra, trigonometry, or any of that stuff. It was with more than average difficulty that I finally conquered the horrifying realm of fractions and algebra.

I gave up trying to comprehend the plethora of fathomless and myriad layers of mathematics of any kind. I cringe when I hear terms such as *Quadratic Equations*, the *Theory of Indices*, *Binomial Theorem*, *Differential Calculus*, *Square Roots*, *Sines*, *Cosines*, and *Tangents*.

After I earned an "A" in ninth grade algebra, I promised myself I would never again take pen or pencil in hand seeking the "correct answer" to any mathematical problem.

My ninth grade algebra teacher, Miss Lilian Blackwell, was as hard-hearted and demanding as anyone I ever met, but she was also dedicated to her teaching profession. She wanted the best for her students, no matter how much she had to make them suffer. No one, to my knowledge, left her classroom without learning something valuable and important.

She held to a single policy that imbued fear

into every student. Although we had a weekly quiz every Friday, we also had a Final Exam at the end of the semester. Nothing mattered except that Final Exam.

A student could get an "A" on every quiz and still fail the Final Exam, which meant you failed the class. Conversely, you could get an "F" on every quiz, but end up with an "A" for the class if you aced the Final Exam. It was, to say the least, unnerving and diabolical. But it worked.

She was one hard nut and she scared the hell out of everybody. Even the "smart girls" in class were stricken with fear in her feminine presence.

In spite of my lack of arithmetic acumen, she was always willing to help me on an individual level, explaining to me (repeatedly) how algebra worked. She deconstructed equations into their smallest parts, examined and explained them, and reconstructed them step-by-step for me so I could understand the machinations of the logic involved. She even went so far as to school me in the concepts of rudimentary logic, which is the rational basis for algebra. For example, a rooster is always a chicken, but a chicken is not always a rooster.

At lease once a week, she would write the acronym *PEMDAS* on the blackboard. She would say, *Please Excuse My Dear Aunt Sally* and demand that the class repeat it. By the end of the semester, it was tattooed into our brains. Stated simply, it's the "order of operations" within algebraic equations. Much later in life, I borrowed her technique to teach this same "order of operations" to computer science students in the San Diego Community College system.

P	Please	Parentheses
E	Excuse	Exponentiation
M	My	Multiplication
D	Dear	Division
A	Aunt	Addition
S	Sally	Subtraction

I continued to muddle my way through the class and near the end of the semester, I had earned a "C" average. My expectations of anything better were becoming more dismal with every quiz. It was especially frustrating since I was pulling a straight "A" in all of my other classes.

One day, a couple of weeks before the semester's end, Miss Blackwell pulled me aside as I was leaving class. She handed me a single sheet of paper and said, "Take this home with you. Keep it in your textbook. Every night, copy everything from this original sheet to another sheet of paper. Look at the original, copy it, and compare the copy to the original. Do you understand?"

I said, "Yes, Ma'am, I'll give it a shot."

She said, "Give it a shot? What type of language is that? Don't give me that nonsense. You do as I tell you and don't give me any excuses. *Every - Single - Night.* Do it"

I took the paper and did as she ordered. It

was horrible. I hated it. But, I did it.

On the day of the final exam she disseminated the mimeographed tests, made sure everyone was ready, and said, "You may commence."

The room became silent. Heads dropped; pencils scribbled, erased, and scribbled again; in a couple of minutes, it was all over.

Okay, it was actually almost an hour, but it seemed like a couple of minutes. The pressure was almost unbearable. I considered jumping out of the third floor window, but thought better of it. If the fall didn't kill me, I'd just be forced to go through it all again. Life can be so harsh.

Very few students finished before the bell rang. Some never finished at all, handing in incomplete exams. I finished about five minutes before the end of class, and I used the extra time to re-examine some of my answers. Much to my surprise, I seemed to know the answers to a few of the questions. Some of them, however, still got the better of me and I guessed at the answers.

As the students exited the classroom, they handed their exams to Miss Blackwell, who was standing next to the door. No one looked her directly in the eye. Some were mumbling to themselves, some were bumping into the walls, and I could swear I heard one kid speaking "in tongues" as he blindly stumbled through the door. A couple of girls seemed to be on the verge of tears. I wasn't feeling too great myself. I handed in my paper, left the room, and expected the worst.

The next day, back in the classroom, Miss Blackwell started the class with the statement, "I will hand your tests back to you. You will see your grade at the top of page one. That will be the grade you receive for the semester. That is also the grade that will go onto your report card. Are there any questions?"

Silence engulfed the earth and the planets momentarily stopped their rotation around the sun. I was certain I felt a shift in the universe. No one asked a question, no one said a word, no one seemed to be breathing.

She continued, "After receiving your tests and having noted your grade for the semester, you may leave. I hope you have learned something during your attendance in my class. I hope you continue to learn as you move forward and attend High School."

We couldn't believe our ears. We were being let out of class early. What sort of madness was this? What sort of adult trickery were we in for? Could this the same teacher who chastised students for being ten seconds late? The same teacher who kept us in class until after the bell stopped ringing? Who made you stand when you asked or answered a question? I was feeling a bit woozy. It was all too much for my amorphous, fifteen year old brain.

I took my Final Exam from her hand and looked at the grade she had written on it. I almost fell out of my seat. She must have made a mistake. I wondered if she knew she had written an "A" on my paper. I wondered if I should say anything. I wondered if I could get away before she realized her error. I was stunned. I sat there going over the paper and looking at every question and answer. My God! I actually understood what I was looking at.

I felt like Helen Keller saying, "Water," for the first time.

It was a couple of minutes before I realized that all the other students had left. I looked up and noticed Miss Blackwell. She was sitting at her desk, watching me.

I threw caution to the wind and said, "Are you sure this is correct? Is this really the right grade?"

She said, "Yes it is. I'm as surprised as you are. It's a good thing you did that extra work the last couple of weeks. You may go now."

I got up and walked to the door. Before leaving, I turned to her and said, "Thank you very much."

She nodded and said, "You're welcome. Remember what you've learned here."

I said, "Yes, Ma'am."

And, that is how I got an "A" in algebra.

* * * * * * * * * * * * * * * * * * * *

It is my firm belief that for every good teacher, there's a bad teacher. If one were to believe in "Dualism" one would understand this as natural and acceptable.

According to Dualism, everything is either Yin or Yang; for example, either the head or the tail of a coin. The intrinsic irony of Yin and Yang is that they co-exist and neither can exist without the other.

If you were to ask me, I'd say, "It's a riddle, wrapped in a mystery, inside an enigma." Okay, I confess to stealing that line from Winston Churchill, but that doesn't make the idea less genuine.

Although I'm unable to offer concrete, tangible proof that Yin and Yang exist, I can certainly offer evidence that there are bad teachers in the educational environment. I shall make my case and let you, dear reader, decide if I am correct.

I had promised myself that after Miss Blackwell's algebra class, I'd never take another "math" class as long as I live. The "school system," however, had different ideas.

I have a faint, fuzzy recollection about Missouri's Department of Secondary Education modifying high school graduation requirements for students taking "college preparatory" classes.

I was told I had to take another math class and by the time I found out about it, the only thing open was trigonometry. Crap on a cracker!

I may not recall the details of how it all came about, but nothing will erase the memory of the ensuing fiasco.

As one can imagine, I was thoroughly disheartened by my dismal prospects; by having to once again enter the murky realm of mathematical endeavors. I truly believed that my excruciating experiences in algebra were the end of my arithmetic agonies. Such was not the case.

"Why?" I asked myself, but I had no answer to offer. I was merely an unsuspecting victim of "the system."

My situation was further exacerbated by the fact that my teacher would be Louis Meyer. I have no knowledge of any student in the history of organized education liking Louis Meyer.

He was referred to as "Mr. Meyer" in his presence, but was otherwise called "Crowman." Our relationship was not only rocky, it was downright rotten from the git-go.

Crowman was as different from Miss Blackwell, my ninth grade algebra teacher, as day is from night, as good is from evil, as right is from wrong, as . . . well, you get the idea.

If my personal experience is any indication, I can truthfully testify that Crowman never, under any circumstances offered the slightest bit of assistance to any student in his class.

He would write strange and cryptic things on the blackboard and tell the students to open the textbook to page such-and-such. He would then assign problems for us to "work out" on our own.

He would pontificate about *Trigonometry Functions, Inverses,* and *Identities* as though they were tangible objects that could be held in one's hand.

He would drone in a monotone about Areas of a *Parallelogram, Angles of Depressions and Elevations, Pythagorean Identities, Double Number Identities, Sum to Difference Identities,*

Tangents, *Laws of Sines and Cosines*, and *Frequencies of Periodic Functions*.

As I sat there on the first day of class, listening to him, the thought occurred to me that, "He sounds like a character from one of those awful science-fiction movies. He's playing his voice backwards to make himself sound like an alien."

And, that is as good as it got. That's also when the trouble started.

Because I failed to comprehend the subject matter, I began to ask questions. The problem was that he would never answer my questions. His response was invariably, "It's in the book. Look in the book."

I would say, "I've looked in the book and I don't understand it. Can you explain it?"

He would say, "I've already explained it. Look in the book."

I would say, "But, I don't understand it. Explain it."

He would say, "I've explained it to the class. You're part of the class. I'm not here to be your personal tutor. Look in the book."

I felt like Lou Costello doing the *Who's On First* routine with Bud Abbott. I have no memory of ever being able to get a straight, sensible answer out of him.

I once asked him, "Why should I look in the book? You're the teacher. You're supposed to teach. If everything's in the book, like you say it is, why do we need a teacher? Aren't you here to explain the subject matter?"

Visibly irritated, he would reply, "I explain things at the start of the class. It's your job to figure out the problems using the textbook. I can't be expected to work out your problems for you. You ask too many questions. You should study the textbook more."

Our relationship as teacher and student continued in this downward spiral until report card time. I stumbled and bumbled my way through the class, trying to get help from some of the other students, but they were too busy "looking in the textbook" to be of any assistance.

When I received my report card, I was hardly surprised when I saw my grade. It was the dreaded "D" that a student gets for simply showing up in class every day. My grade in every other class was a straight "A."

That, however, wasn't the worst part. Reading the report card, I saw a note, in Crowman's handwriting, at the bottom of the third page. It said, "Province is lazy and doesn't try at all. He talks too much and constantly interrupts class."

I was appalled. I read it a couple more times and said under my breath, "Jesus H. Christ, the only time I talk is when I ask a question. This is a bunch of bullshit."

I was genuinely angry and I swore to return the favor. The next day, I came to school with a plan.

I attended my morning classes, as usual, and was sitting in the library during my "Study Hall" class. That's when I made my move.

Students normally used Study Hall to work

on class assignments and extra homework, but I wouldn't be doing that today.

I ambled to the corner door of the library which was directly opposite the door into Crowman's classroom. I pretended to use the pencil sharpener on the wall as I surveyed his classroom. I ran a scenario through my mind and practiced my part in the upcoming drama.

I knew his routine, so I waited until I saw him walk to his desk at the back of the room where he always sat and fiddled around while his students worked on their assigned problems and "looked in the textbook."

I slid my pencil into my shirt pocket, took my report card in hand, and strolled across the hallway.

I quietly opened the door to his classroom, leaving it wide open, and I walked in.

I thrust my report card in front of his face and said quite loudly, "I want to know why you wrote all this junk on my report card. What kind of teacher are you?"

He was plainly startled and blurted out, "How dare you? Get out! You're interrupting my class."

I said, "I'm not leaving until you explain to me what you mean by this crud you wrote. It's not bad enough you won't teach me anything, now you have to screw up my report card, too."

Recovering a little, he said, "I wrote that because it's my opinion."

I offered the card to him and said, "Then write another note that it's only your opinion and that it doesn't matter."

He became quite flustered. He stood up and yelled, "Get out of here! You have no right to be here!"

We went round-and-round and back-and-forth like this for a few minutes and every time I spoke, it was louder than before. Soon enough, I was yelling, demanding that he mark out what he had written on my report card. I admit that I eventually used some rather "inappropriate language" during our discussion.

Glancing to the left, I noticed that across the hallway, in the library, at least a dozen students were lined up waiting to "sharpen" their pencils. They seemed to be enjoying the show. Other teachers had left their classrooms and were congregating in the hallway, watching us and listening to the shouting match between Crowman and me.

Mrs. Vaughn walked into the hallway, watched us for a minute, and then entered Crowman's classroom. She took a position directly between us, separating us, and said, "Please lower your voices. You're disturbing the other classes."

She spoke to Crowman, saying, "You should be ashamed. You're a teacher. You should know better."

She turned to me and said, "Michael, I think we've all gotten your point. Will you please come with me?"

Fuming, I stood there for a few more seconds before I let out a breath and said, "Sure. I'm sick of looking at him anyway. As Grandpa would say, 'He's as useless as tits on a boar hog.' "

From the look on his face, I'm certain Crowman wanted to punch me in the mouth after that remark.

Mrs. Vaughn said, "That's enough! Stop it right now."

She escorted me downstairs to the first floor and into the principal's office where she asked me to sit down.

She spoke to the secretary, "I need to see Dr. Simmons - immediately."

The secretary picked up her phone, punched a button, spoke in a hushed voice, and said, "Dr. Simmons will see you. Please go in, Mrs. Vaughn."

She entered his office, stayed long enough to make me wonder what they were saying to each other, and when she came out she said to me, "I can appreciate your frustrations, but there are far better ways to handle this type of situation. Your father has been contacted and will be here soon. Dr. Simmons will be waiting to talk to both of you."

I said, "Yeah, a lot of good that'll do. Why don't they just kick me out of school right now?"

Shaking her head, she said, "No one is going to kick you out of school. I've explained what little I know about your situation and Dr. Simmons is willing to listen to your side of the story. Is that agreeable?"

I began to calm down a little and said, "Yeah, I guess so."

"Good," she said, "Your father should be here

soon."

As she walked away, I said, "Mrs. Vaughn?"

Turning toward me she said, "Yes?"

I said, "Thank you. I appreciate your help. You're one of the few people who listen to me."

She smiled, turned, and headed upstairs to finish the short time left in her Speech Arts class.

About a half-hour later, the old man showed up. He wasn't happy, but, what the hell, neither was I.

We were quickly ushered into the principal's office where Dr. Simmons asked us to make ourselves comfortable.

I was asked to explain my problem. By that time, although I was still angry, I was no longer looking for a fight. For the next fifteen minutes, I explained my predicament to Dr. Simmons, who listened patiently without interrupting me.

I gave him my unvarnished opinion of Crowman, excuse me, *Mr. Meyer* and threw in, free of charge, my opinion of his so-called teaching methods.

I finished with the comment, "I'm sick and tired of this whole mess. If you want to expel me, go ahead. I don't care. I thought schools were supposed to help students but, if not, I'll just quit and go find a crappy job somewhere. Everybody else in my family works in the lead mines, there's no reason why I can't, too."

Dr. Simmons said, "I don't believe any of that will be necessary. You are correct in your assessment of the necessity of the school system to assist the student in performing to the best of his or her ability and to prepare them for a good, decent life."

"We do, in fact, possess a certain amount of latitude regarding the requirements for graduation. I would like for you to work with our school counselor to discuss the various avenues available to you. I will personally instruct him to work with you to devise a program to continue with your college preparatory levels. You have my promise that you will be involved in every step of the process. Furthermore, we will finalize your individualized program only when you agree to it."

"I also have at my disposal, the authority to ease the transition from your current problematical class into something more helpful and useful to you. Would this be acceptable to you?"

I sat there, digesting his comments and giving his offer some serious thought.

I said to the old man, "What do you think?"

He said, "It's your decision. I'm behind you whatever you decide."

I said, "What about my grades? The grade he put on my report card is going to mess up my grade point average. Can anything be done about that?"

He appeared to be very sincere when he said, "I am extremely sorry, but once the grade is recorded, it cannot be altered. Transcripts are, unfortunately, immutable. Please consider this, however. I can provide to you my personal guarantee that Mr. Meyer will be informed of the situation he has created for you and my conversation with him will go into his "permanent" record. So, in a sense, he will be given a "poor grade" in the same manner he has given you a "poor grade." It will, in fact, have an effect on his next efficiency report, and his overall competence assessment."

I said, "So he'll get sort of a "report card" like I did? One that reflects his . . . deficiencies? And, once it's on his record, it can't be changed?"

Dr. Simmons smiled and said, "Yes, that could be the lay person's explanation of what will happen. Once the information is entered into his personal file, it cannot be expunged."

At the end of the meeting, the old man and I left Dr. Simmon's office and walked out to his car without saying a word. Before he left I said, "You didn't say much in there."

He said, "I didn't need to. You were doing okay without me. To tell you the truth, Mike, I think you're smarter than me. You just have some growing up to do, that's all. You're gonna be out on your own pretty soon anyway. You don't need me to fight your fights."

I said, "Thanks, Pop. I appreciate that."

Then something odd happened. We hugged each other, just like we did when I was a little kid.

As it turned out, Dr. Simmons' promise was as good as gold. The latitude given to me in my math "requirements" allowed me to work on my own in Study Hall.

I completed my class using a "programmed instruction" textbook. I was one of the guinea pigs for a new *educational technology* invented in 1954 at Harvard University by B.F. Skinner, the behaviorial psychologist.

Oddly enough, I used the same type of textbook instruction to learn IBM's Autocoder Programming language when I worked at the Trimfoot Shoe Company.

I wish I could report that my grade point average turned out okay, but that was not to be. I still had difficulty with trigonometry, but I was at least able to pull a "C+" for the class. That, plus the grade Crowman gave me, caused me to graduate with a "B" average instead of the "A" average I had maintained throughout high school. It also kept me out of the Honor Society.

On the plus side of the equation (snicker, snicker) I never had to enter Crowman's classroom again. I'm sure he was just as glad about that as I was.

I found out many years later that he "retired" a couple of years after our confrontation. I wonder if our little "disagreement" had anything to do with it.

I think he had been teaching too long; he was bored; he was tired of teaching; he didn't want to expend any effort, and he didn't want to do anything except cash his paychecks. I've seen that happen to a lot of teachers. I know because I was a college teacher for fifteen years.

Within the last decade, a learning disability

known as *dyscalculia* has been discovered. It's similar to dyslexia, but involves the inability to learn mathematics. Luckily, neither dyslexia nor dyscalculia affect the true intelligence of an individual.

I sometimes wonder if that's what my problem was (and still is). At my age, though, it doesn't really matter, does it?

Postscript

In 1968, I was living in Ocean Beach, a suburb of San Diego. Down the street from my tiny apartment was a little bar called *Edna's Leilani Club*.

I was sitting on a barstool at Edna's one Saturday night and after having a few brews I began to think about Mathematics.

In a flash, I saw it all, depth beyond depth was revealed to me, both the negative and the positive of the universe. I envisioned a numerical quantity passing through infinity and altering its sign from plus to minus. I saw and understood exactly how and why it happened and why the tergiversation was universally inevitable; I could see and understand how one step involved all the succeeding steps. All of mathematics was clearly, distinctly, and precisely revealed to me at that moment.

And then . . . it was gone.

So I had another beer.

Above: *Left*; Flat River Junior College and High School. *Right*; Flat River Junior High School. *Right-Rear*; Assembly Hall.

Below: Flat River Junior College and High School. The classroom in the upper-right corner is where the confrontation with Louis "Crowman" Meyer took place.

Above: A rare picture of Flat River Junior High School where I aced my algebra class.

Below: In 1968, *Edna's Leilani Club* was next to the coin laundry. I spent many Saturday evenings there contemplating the universe. I wonder what's there today.

The Case of the Stupid State Trooper and Other Cop-Shop Stories

I was on the way to work at Trimfoot one Saturday morning when I stopped by the old man's house to see what he was up to.

I was scheduled spend the weekend "defragmenting" the RAMAC Disk Storage device connected to our IBM 1401 Computer System. The owner of the company had an expansive, "live in" office apartment, which he used as living quarters when he visited from his home in St. Louis. I would be sleeping on the overstuffed sofa Saturday night so I could be sure to get the job done before Monday morning. I learned to write computer programs on that machine.

Defragmentation of a hard disk in today's personal computers is a simple, quick, and minor operation, but in the days of "big iron" mainframe computers, "defragging" was a massive, difficult, and time consuming process.

The RAMAC magnetic storage system consisted of a stack of fifty 24-inch disks. The center hole in a single disk was large enough to put your head through, if you needed to do such a thing.

The storage capacity of the disk system was 5,000,000 *7-bit characters* which was specifically

6 *data-bits* and 1 *parity-check-bit*. Among the "in crowd" RAMAC's storage capacity was referred to as 5-Megabytes. In simple terms, the letter "A" (or any other letter of the alphabet) could be stored 5,000,000 times. It was one of the last systems to use vacuum tubes and it weighed over a ton. Another way to explicate storage capacity would be to say that we could store about 64,000 "80-column" punch cards.

That may be sadly unimpressive compared to today's 64-Gigabyte flash drive on a keychain, but at the time it was cutting edge technology; an amazing feat of scientific and mechanical ingenuity. Without it, there would be no flash drives dangling from keychains.

Trimfoot purchased the IBM 1401 for the paltry sum of $750,000. Perhaps I should mention that RAMAC stands for *Random Access Method of Accounting and Control*. That could be crucial if you're ever on Jeopardy.

A heavily fragmented disk system was a danger to itself. About every six months, the stored data had been randomly written and deleted to such an extent the read/write access arm began to slide up-and-down and in-and-out so quickly and severely, it was literally beating itself to death. On certain access operations the machine would bounce back and forth like a washing machine with an unbalanced load of laundry.

Although defragmentation was an arduous task, it can be explained rather simply. First, I programmed the computer to punch cards for every record we had on the disk drive. This usually amounted to 30-to-40 thousand cards.

Next, I sorted those cards into the proper sequence. This took hours and required the cards to be stacked and organized into their proper "sorting sequence." During this phase, I had every desk in the office covered with stacks of cards.

After the cards were re-sequenced, I began loading them back onto the RAMAC. The access arm would write the records starting at the top with track 1 of cylinder 1 of disk 1. It would then make its way down the stack of disks until they were all in perfect sequence.

At that point, the machine would access information quickly and efficiently. There was only one problem; with the first daily processing activity, the disk would begin fragmenting the data again and a few months later, the "defrag" would need to be repeated.

So much for my weekend plans at Trimfoot.

I parked in front of the old man's house, got out, walked up the driveway and onto his tiny porch. I knocked on the door and heard him say, "There's no one home."

I opened the door, walked in, and said, "I'm glad there's nobody here, now I can ransack this lousy dump and steal them blind."

"Sorry," said the old man, "we ain't got nuthin' to steal. I got me some eggs in the icebox, though."

I said, "Maybe later. Whatcha watchin' ?"

My question was purely rhetorical. I knew

what he was watching; re-runs of cartoons. The old man really liked old cartoon shows, especially the one currently gracing the screen of his 21-inch color television.

"Queeks Draw," He said, referring to *Quick Draw McGraw*.

He pronounced it with a heavy Mexican accent because that's the way *Baba Looey* pronounced it. Baba Looey was Quick Draw's sidekick-deputy, a little Mexican burro.

The old man also had an affinity for the cartoon duo of *Augie Doggie* and *Doggie Daddy*; dachshunds who shared a number of misadventures, most of which were caused by Doggie Daddy.

The old man was sometimes known to actually quote these characters if a situation merited such wisdom. His favorite *Queeks Draw* quote was, "I'll do the thin'in (*thinking*) aroun' here! And, don't you fer-git it!" I think the cartoonists may have been stolen that from Ricky Ricardo.

I sat down and watched the rest of the show with him and for some reason, couldn't help but laugh at some of the silliness. Things were funnier back then.

At the end of the show, he shut off the television and said, "You should'a been at the jail a couple of nights ago. We had a bit of excitement."

I said, "Bueno, Queeks Draw. Que pasó, amigo?"

"Well," he said, "first off you need to know

that we have a new state trooper in the area. He's young, inexperienced, and a bit stupid. He doesn't follow procedure and this time it got him into a hell of a lot of trouble."

"Why am I not surprised," I interjected, "I wonder if he's a college graduate."

"Yeah," said the old man, "I wonder, too. Anyhow, he pulled over a drunk driver who smelled like a brewery. The guy had an open can of beer in his hand while he was asking why he had been pulled over. In spite of all that, the trooper wasted a lot of time and trouble giving him a sobriety test. You know, walk heel to toe, and all that crap."

"Why didn't he just cuff him and bring him in," I enquired.

"Like I said, because he's not very bright, that's why," reflected the old man.

"So, what happened then?" I asked.

"He put the guy in the back seat of his patrol car and brought him to the jail for the purpose of incarceration," said the old man as he smiled.

"The trouble was," he continued, "he said the guy was joking around and being all *friendly like* so he didn't think he posed any threat. He failed to cuff him and he forgot to search him for weapons."

"Geez, what a nimrod," I nodded.

The old man said, "So, he drove him to the jail, brought him inside, and told him we were going to hold him for the night so he could sober up. We were going to let him go the next morning, but that's when things started to go wrong."

I shook my head and said, "I can imagine."

The old man said, "Yeah, the trouble with a drunk is he can turn on you in a second and get meaner than a wet hen. That's what this guy did. He told the trooper to go fuck himself, said he wasn't staying in our stinking jail, and he pulled a little .22 automatic out of his pants pocket."

"Yeah," I said, "I can see how that would be pretty exciting. Did anybody get hurt?"

"Both of 'em got hurt," said the old man, "the drunk aimed the gun at the trooper, the trooper grabbed the gun trying to get it away from him, and the drunk shot him through the hand. I grabbed my big billy club and hit him as hard as I could behind his right ear. I must have looked like Stan Musial. I was swinging as hard as I could when I connected with his head. I heard him grunt, he went down on his knees, but he tried to get up again."

"Boy, he must have been one tough bastard," I said, "of course drunks don't feel much anyway."

"That was part of the problem," said the old man, "he was just a little guy, but he wasn't feeling any pain. I raised the club over my head and brought it down on top of his thick skull. At that moment, it was my intention to kill the little son-of-a-bitch. The second whack got him. His arms flopped down, he dropped the gun, and he tipped over onto his face. He hit the concrete floor so hard he broke his nose, too. Serves him right. I looked at the billy club later and it was bent. And that thing has an inch thick hunk of lead inside the leather wrapping."

I asked, "Did you kill him?"

"That's the funny part," said the old man, "other than being knocked out, he was okay. I dragged him into a cell, took his belt and shoes along with his personal items, threw a blanket over him, and locked the door. The next morning he woke up complaining of a headache and he didn't remember what he did. He was joking around, asking for breakfast, and wanting to know when he could pay his fine and get back on the road."

I said, "Are you telling me he had no memory of anything that happened and other than a headache, he was perfectly fine?"

"Yeah," said the old man, "Ain't that weird? Ken (Sheriff Buckley) was in the upstairs living quarters with his wife when he heard the shot and he ran downstairs immediately. I told him what happened and he said he was going to make sure the prosecuting attorney was present when they told the guy about shooting the trooper. They're going to charge him with attempted murder."

"That's crazy," I said, "he could have just spent the night in jail and now he's looking at ten to twenty years in prison."

The old man shook his head and said, "Nah, I doubt it. That's not the way our so-called justice system works. The prosecuting attorney will talk to the defense attorney, they'll argue for a little while, then they'll "agree" that since he was drunk he didn't know what he was doing. They'll let him plea bargain to a charge of attempted involuntary manslaughter and give him a year in jail with probation. With good behavior, he could be out in six months. That way both attorneys can count it as a win. The prosecutor gets his conviction and the defense attorney gets his man off with the least amount of time served.

It works especially well for our dear prosecuting attorney, *Mr. Roberts*. All he cares about is getting a conviction on his record."

I said, "In spite of the trying to shoot a cop?"

"Well, you gotta consider," continued the old man, "the trooper ignored proper procedure. I can see a defense attorney arguing that because of the trooper's incompetence, the situation was allowed to get out of hand. Nobody wants the trooper to have to testify. It would be embarrassing for him to say the least. I know a couple of attorneys who would love to get him on the stand. They'd rip him apart. All he had to do was cuff the guy and search him, but he didn't. That's not only incompetent, it's just plain stupid."

"Yeah, there's a reason people say you can never trust a drunk," I said, "and every time he looks at his hand, he'll be reminded of what he should have done. Like they say, 'Lessons hard learned are lessons well learned.' "

"Ain't that the truth?" said the old man, "are you sure you don't want me to fry you up some eggs?"

"No, thanks," I said, "I gotta get going. Those cards aren't gonna sort themselves, you know."

I pointed my finger at the old man and said, "Try not to get killed, okay?"

As I walked out the door, I heard him say, "I'm not planning on it, but if I do, I'll sure as hell take somebody with me."

I said, "Good idea, make it worth your while. You know, if you don't want to be shot at, you shouldn't be a deputy sheriff."

"I know," said the old man, "but the money's good and we've already talked about that."

I nodded my head and said, "Yeah, life's full of risks no matter what you do. Nobody gets out alive, do they?"

I closed the door, walked to my car, and drove about a mile to the Trimfoot building. I wasn't looking forward to the weekend, but at least I would be alone and wouldn't be bothered by anyone. And, it was good overtime pay.

When I first started this episode, I planned on stopping right about now, but memories have resurfaced concerning my involvement with the Sheriff's Office. I think I'll continue.

Ken Buckley was a good man. He was well liked in the community, and, in my opinion, he was perhaps the best Sheriff St. Francois County ever had. He was certainly the longest serving Sheriff in the history of the office. He was elected to five terms of office; 1964-68, 1968-72, 1972-76, 1980-84, and 1984-88 term; a total of twenty years.

He probably would have been re-elected to

the 1976-80 term, but he encountered political difficulties. Small town politics is very rough game and in Ken's case, politics interrupted his law enforcement career.

As he started his first term as Sheriff, Buckley immediately experienced problems with the county's prosecuting attorney, Hugh C. Roberts, Jr.

According to my old man, Roberts thought he was God's gift to the legal profession. He brought arrogance, egotism, and hubris to a new level. Roberts held the opinion that the sheriff's department existed solely for his benefit and a sheriff who disagreed had to be punished.

Roberts' legal posture depended on who was paying him. Essentially, he was your average lawyer . . . a hypocrite of immense proportions.

As prosecuting attorney, Roberts strove against all odds to put criminals behind bars where those evil-doers belonged.

As a lawyer in private practice, Roberts strove against all odds to protect those same individuals who were now poor, downtrodden, and misunderstood victims of an egalitarian legal system violating their rights and vilifying their reputations.

Buckley, however, was his own man with his own opinions. He refused to be bullied and intimidated by the prosecuting attorney.

Buckley and Roberts disliked each other professionally and personally, and they didn't mind who knew it. Their relationship was a disaster just waiting to happen. The ill feelings between the two men created a rift that could not and would not be bridged.

Roberts' vendetta against Buckley began in 1972 when he initiated an agenda of dirty tricks aimed at getting rid of the sheriff once and for all, no matter what it took. When Roberts began to push, Buckley pushed back.

One of the despicable stunts Roberts pulled involved the extradition of a fugitive named Roy Durain. The old man told me about it.

Durain was charged with stealing an amount of money over $50 (a felony), neglecting to pay a local motel bill of more than $500 (another felony), and stealing a car from a Farmington automobile leasing company (yet another felony). He had been released on his own cognizance but failed to appear in court so a Capias Warrant had been issued for his immediate arrest.

It was learned through law enforcement channels that Durain was being held in a county jail in Green River, Wyoming so prosecuting attorney Roberts contacted Missouri Governor Christopher Bond, requesting an extradition warrant. The warrant was issued and signed by both the Missouri Governor and the Wyoming Governor, Ed Herschler.

Roberts requested that Sheriff Buckley send a couple of deputies to Wyoming to pick up the alleged felon, which Buckley did. The problem developed when the two deputies arrived at the county jail in Green River. The deputies drove 2,600 miles round trip to pick up the prisoner but upon their arrival at the jail, they were informed that the prisoner had been released.

When questioned about the incident, Roberts stated that, "He was contacted by a Wyoming judge to arrange for Durain to make restitution to the auto leasing agency and the motel." Roberts claimed he had agreed to the request because the Wyoming officials told him Durain had found a $1,000 a month job. The Missouri charges for which the prisoner was extradited and the extradition warrant were legally pending when Durain was released, but Roberts ignored the warrant.

Roberts never explained why he failed to let the Sheriff know about the release, claiming it was all just an unfortunate misunderstanding. He feigned innocence, saying he had not "engineered" the release as a prank against the Sheriff. He said he was simply trying to help another human being. It was just one of many "dirty tricks" Roberts pulled on Buckley throughout his vendetta.

Buckley, as one can imagine, was fed up with Roberts and his petulant antics. He contacted Circuit Court Judge J. O. Swink and demanded that a special prosecutor be named to investigate the actions of the prosecuting attorney, his incompetence, his disregard for the law, and dereliction of duty.

The old man told me, "What happened next does little to improve my opinion of lawyers."

A special prosecutor was never named in the extradition matter, but Roberts had been embarrassed by the publicity and he took the vendetta to a new level of legal mockery. He was not above using his position as prosecuting attorney nor his political connections in Jefferson City (the state capitol) to attack Sheriff Buckley.

In 1973, Buckley deputized his wife's uncle, Fred Fisher, as a process-server for the Sheriff's office. When Roberts learned of the appointment, he filed a petition with Missouri's Supreme Court calling for the ouster of Sheriff Buckley on the grounds of nepotism.

Buckley asserted that the petition was false, malicious, and politically motivated. His attorney filed a petition with the Supreme Court requesting that Roberts' petition be dismissed because the circuit judge, J.O. Swink, approved the appointment. Buckley held the opinion that Fisher was not a blood relative and if the appointment violated the constitutional provision, the circuit court judge would have, and should have forbidden it.

To put a fine point on it, Buckley claimed he actually did not appoint Fisher. He said that the circuit court appointed Fisher upon the Sheriff's recommendation.

Unfortunately, the Missouri State Supreme court sided with Roberts. Their "opinion" declared that Buckley's relationship to Fisher, even though it was through marriage, was the same as a blood relative. Buckley, they said, would have to forfeit his office. The text of the court's opinion was: "It is ordered that the respondent is ousted from the office of sheriff of

St. Francois County until the end of his present term expiring December 31, 1976, and the costs of this proceeding are taxed against him. All concur."

Upon his removal, Buckley was replaced by his deputy, James Hickman, who was appointed to serve the unexpired term. Buckley sat out the next sheriff's race but won re-election for the 1980-84 and 1984-88 terms.

Okay, one last little episode, and I'll end this chapter.

I was discharged from the army and returned to Flat River in 1965. By that time Ken had been serving as Sheriff for a year and a half and the old man had been sworn in as one of Ken's deputies. I was out of work and looking for almost any sort of employment. Since I had a lot of time on my hands, Ken was good enough to help me out occasionally.

From time to time, county jail prisoners were required to be transported to and from other counties and to the State Penitentiary in Jefferson City, Missouri's capitol. I was deputized a few times as a temporary guard to accompany a full time deputy during some of these trips. I was paid a flat "per diem" fee which was very helpful at that point in my life. For the most part, these trips were uneventful, but one, in particular, sticks in my mind.

There was a young punk who thought he was a real tough guy. In reality, he was a two-bit thief and burglar who had been in and out of jail for petty crimes a number of times.

This time, however, he had escalated his crimes. He had gotten drunk and broke into a house where a nice old lady lived. Realizing she had nothing to steal, he began to smack her around and ended up beating her quite badly. He didn't kill her but she was hospitalized for a couple of weeks. At his trial he made the plea that he didn't know what he was doing because he had too much to drink.

Now, where I come from, that sort of thing doesn't sit well with folks. Nobody needs to beat up a nice little old lady and being drunk is no excuse.

The smarmy, sleazy little hood was given a fair trial, a jury found him guilty, the prosecuting attorney suggested the maximum penalty, and the judge sentenced him to a minimum of ten years in the state penitentiary. Because it was a conviction for first-degree-assault the judge could have sentenced him for a longer period, but ten years is a very long time behind bars.

On the day of his transportation, I was duly sworn in as a deputy and I was told he was a sneaky little bastard who would take a cheap shot at you if he could manage it. My old man took a small 25-caliber, 9-shot automatic pistol out of his pocket, slipped the magazine into the grip, and pulled back the slide to chamber a round.

He handed it to me and said, "You know how to handle this. Take it and keep it handy. Do NOT use it unless YOUR life is in danger."

I said, "Okay. I won't need it, but it'll be nice to have just in case something does happen."

He patted me on the shoulder and said, "I'll see you this evening." He turned and walked into the Sheriff's office.

The prisoner was brought out manacled at his hands and feet with a chain between the two. We assisted him into the backseat of the patrol car, the deputy sheriff got behind the wheel, and we headed down the road toward the state penitentiary in Jefferson City. I think I'll refer to the deputy as "Deputy Dawg" since I don't want to use his real name. I will admit I didn't like him from the start.

We had just gotten onto the highway when the prisoner started talking, and he wouldn't shut up. He bitched and whined about the woman he beat up, the deputies who arrested him, the judge, the jury, the prosecuting attorney, his wife, his parents, and on and on. According to him, everybody in the world was against him, he never had a decent chance in life, he was always being picked on by the cops. You name it, he had a reason for it. Everything bad that happened to him was somebody else's fault.

Halfway to Jefferson City, I turned to Deputy Dawg and said, "I'm really sick of this guy."

He nodded and said, "Yeah, he's a real pain in the ass."

We drove for a few more minutes before Deputy Dawg said, "I got an idea. Watch this."

I didn't like the sound of that.

He pulled the car off the highway and onto a gravel road, then onto a smaller road into a thick area of woods. He stopped the car and said, "I need to take a leak. How about you, Mike, do you need to take a leak?"

I said, "Yes, I believe I do."

We "exited the vehicle" (cop talk for got out of the car) and stood on opposite sides of the car while we relieved ourselves.

Deputy Dawg said, "I'm going to teach this bastard a lesson."

I said, "I'm not going to be a party to any rough stuff. Let's just get back on the road and get this over with."

Deputy Dawg said, "Nah, no rough stuff, I'm just gonna pull a little trick on him, that's all. It'll be funny."

I was liking him less and less as the moments went by and I began to worry about him being completely nuts. I said, "Let's get back on the road. I don't need this kind of crap."

Deputy Dawg went behind the car, extracted the bullets from his revolver, and put the pistol back in his holster.

He walked to the rear door of the patrol car, opened it, and looked at the prisoner. He said, "I'm sick and tired of you and your motor mouth, boy. Now I'm gonna give you one chance. You can promise me that you'll shut up the rest of the trip, or I'm gonna shoot your brains out."

The prisoner's eyes got huge and he said, "I'll talk if I want to. You can't shut me up. You're full of shit. You wouldn't shoot me."

Deputy Dawg said, "Well, now, there you go. Ya see, I gave you a chance, boy, and you messed it up."

The prisoner started screaming, "Hey! I've got rights. You can't treat me like this! I've got rights, damnit!"

I watched as Deputy Dawg pulled his revolver and aimed it at the prisoner's head.

I yelled at him, "Get back in the God-damned car!"

The prisoner began to curse, scream, and beg before he became very quiet.

I heard the gun click. The prisoner jerked and cringed. He almost whispered, "Okay, okay, I'll be quiet. I'll be quiet."

Deputy Dawg smiled and said, "Now remember, boy, a promise is a promise."

He reloaded his revolver, slipped it back in its holster, and we continued our journey.

The prisoner never said another word. Neither did I.

Arriving at the penitentiary we walked him through the heavy steel doors and into the prison. We checked our guns with the guards and then went through two more sets of steel-barred doors, ending up at a desk where a prison guard accepted the prisoner's incarceration papers.

The manacles were removed from the prisoner and two guards took him by the arms and "escorted" him through two more sets of steel-barred doors. All the doors were electric and a guard on the "outside" of each door had to push a button to open the next door.

By this time I was almost feeling sorry for the guy. I looked around and thought to myself, "Maybe Deputy Dawg would be doing him a favor to put a bullet in his head."

I immediately put that thought out of my head. The prisoner had caused his own problems and ended up here because of his own decisions. Everybody makes their own choices.

That still didn't give Deputy Dawg the right to do what he did. There was no need for it and it was wrong.

As I was wondering what the prisoner would be like after ten years in this place, I caught a final glimpse of him just before he turned the corner into the bowels of the prison. He looked back and saw me watching him. I could almost see the fear dripping from his face.

Before I got back into the patrol car, I looked around at the prison and thought to myself, "This place is evil."

As Deputy Dawg started the engine he said, "Fer Crissakes, it was just a damn joke."

It was a very quiet ride back to Farmington. I didn't say a word to Deputy Dawg during the entire trip. When we arrived, the old man had already finished his shift and had gone home.

I drove to his house, gave him his little automatic pistol, and told him everything that happened. I said, "I'm done. Somebody else can help transport your prisoners. I don't want any part of this shit any more."

"I understand," said the old man, "when I

started this job, I told Ken I'd work the Dispatcher's Desk, but that's it."

A few days later the old man told me Deputy Dawg had been fired.

It's been fifty years since I made the trip to that evil place. I wonder what happened to that prisoner.

The first disk drive. The defragmenation process was excruciatingly horrible.

The old man is "armed and dangerous" in front of the St. Francois County Jail.

The St. Francois County Jail, with living quarters above and the jail below. It was freezing in the winter and sweltering in the summer.

The Missouri State Penitentiary, in Jefferson City, was also known as "The Walls." It opened in 1836 and until it closed in 2004 was the oldest operational penal facility west of the Mississippi River.

Poor Little Cuddles

Memory is an intriguing thing. I had received an email from my favorite nephew, John Province, who lives in Spring Valley, California, a suburb of beautiful San Diego. Out of the blue, a vision appeared in my mind of his little dog, *Cuddles*. Thinking of Cuddles reminded me of when and why I moved to California in 1967. In retrospect, it seems so complicated now.

1965 and 1966 turned out to be very busy years for the Province Clan.

I had been discharged from the army in 1965 and was living with the old man in Farmington, Missouri. He and Ellen were renting a small place just a couple of blocks from the *Trimfoot Shoe Company.*

Before I got settled in, we made quick a trip to Madison, Wisconsin to attend my brother Harold's wedding. He married a girl named Mitzi Hamilton whom he met while attending the University of Missouri. She had been going to Stephens College but she opted to marry Harold instead of finishing school.

I was doing my best to make my living arrangements as temporary as possible. I was submitting employment applications and resumés at every business in the Lead Belt that might use my expertise in the operation of IBM punch card machines. That's what I had been trained for in the army and that's what I wanted to do for a living. It was better than digging ditches.

My job search was looking bleak, so I asked Aunt Theresa if I might be able to stay with her and Uncle Herman while I looked for a job in St. Louis. They agreed and I spent a month in a tiny room in their attic while I wore out a lot of shoe leather, filled out innumerable employment application forms, and combed the daily want ads in the *St. Louis Post Dispatch*.

The job search was no better in St. Louis, so I decided to return to the Lead Belt and accept any job that was available. Through a friend of a friend of my old man, I found out about a job at the IGA store in Rivermines. I made a quick trip over there and applied for the job. I was offered the job of bag boy. I didn't care for the sound of the job title, but it was money in my pocket so I couldn't complain.

I showed up on time, worked hard, was polite to the customers, and did everything that was asked of me. Then the ax came down.

I had the job for a little over a month when I was told by another employee that the manager wanted to see me in his office at the end of my shift.

I met him at the appointed time and place and I knew it was going to be bad when he said, "You've been a good worker but things have changed."

Realizing he was about to fire me, I asked him, "What is it, exactly, that I've done wrong?"

His answer was hardly what I was expecting. He explained, "You haven't done anything wrong. It's just that I have a niece who's moving to the area and she needs a job. So, I'm going to have to let you go to make room for her. After all, family is family. Besides, I just needed somebody to fill in for the past month until she got here. Sorry about that, kid."

He offered me a check for the amount he owed me and I accepted it.

I said, "You know something. I probably should be angry, but I'm not. You want to know why?"

I didn't give him a chance to respond since it was a purely rhetorical question.

I said, "I had to put up with a lot of rotten assholes in the army but I don't have to do that now. I don't want to work for you because you're an asshole, too. You could have told me it was a temporary job."

I turned around and walked out of his office, looking back at him for a few seconds with my hand on the door knob.

I said, "And, don't call me kid, you Jackass," then I pulled the door shut with such a slam it shook the windows in his office.

I drove to the bank where I deposited the check, just in case he might try to stop payment on it. People can be jerks about things like that.

Then I drove straight to the Employment Office and filed for unemployment. I've never understood why the government calls those places "employment offices." I've never known anyone who ever found a job there.

I went home and told the old man what happened. He said, "Good for you. I never liked that son-of-a-bitch anyway."

I matriculated at Flat River Junior College and continued to draw unemployment for a semester while I attended classes. One semester is all I completed before my education was put on hold.

I received a phone call from the manager of computer operations at the Trimfoot Shoe Company in Farmington. He offered me a job as second shift supervisor and I accepted the offer.

I went to work at Trimfoot and ran the evening shift operations. When the business office shut down for the day, my crew and I processed the day's baby shoe orders and I ran all the requisite daily, weekly, and monthly business reports.

The company had an IBM 1401 Computer System, several keypunch machines, an electronic sorter, a card collator, and a card interpreter. It was a very nice little system. I was told they had bought the system for about a quarter of a million dollars. It had less operating power than the Macintosh I'm using to write this.

A week later I got a call from Aunt Theresa. She said the folks at the Anheuser-Busch brewery called her asking for me. They were interested in offering me a job. I called the number she gave me and explained to the personnel officer that I had accepted a job near my home town. I thanked her for the offer. It doesn't cost anything to show appreciation, you know.

Unbelievably, the next week I got a third phone call, this time from the St. Joe Lead Company and they offered me a job. Three job offers in three weeks. Hard to believe, but true. I thanked them for their offer but explained that I had accepted a position with Trimfoot. They wished me luck and little did I know I might need it.

As soon as I got my first paycheck, I moved out of the old man's house. According to Ellen, I had worn out my welcome. She said she was "uncomfortable" with me around. I was more than happy to comply with her wishes.

Unfortunately, my presence had created some ill feelings between her and the old man. They broke up shortly after I left their house.

I had been living in a drafty old house on Blue Goose Hill for about a week when I heard a car pull into my driveway. Looking out the window, I saw the old man walking toward the house. He came in without knocking and said he needed someplace to stay for a while. I showed him the extra bedroom and said, "Make yourself at home."

It was lucky for both of us that it was a furnished house. The beds weren't great, but beggars can't be choosers.

What I remember most about that house was

the lack of heat. There was a small gas heater in the front room which was far from adequate. I was always cold in that house. The single winter I lived there, I thought for sure I was going to freeze to death. It was worse than the German winters in the Army.

By the time spring was near, the old man came in one day and said, "Ellen and I have sort of patched things up. We're going to buy a little place in Farmington. We'll be moving into the house in a week or so." The little house they bought was at 202 North Alexander Street. It's also where I saw him for the last time in 1978. He was dying of cancer and I spent a week with him there. He died a few days after I left.

I offered him my congratulations, still wondering what in the world he saw in that woman. She was as slow as molasses and she smelled like an ash tray.

My immediate reaction to his news was to start searching for a small house of my own. I found one at the corner of Coffman Street and Wilson Street in Flat River.

To get there, I would drive past the Roseland Theater, the Taxi Stand, the Baptist and Methodist churches, and down Coffman's steep hill. The house was at the bottom of the hill just as Coffman curved sharply to the left.

When it rained, there was a small river in the back of the property, which emptied into Flat River Creek. I had to constantly check the sump pump in the basement to make sure the place wouldn't be flooded.

When it snowed, it was a dangerous place to either get in to or out of.

I paid $5000 for it and I think I was cheated. Live and learn.

I worked at Trimfoot for around a year-and-a-half before I began to have trouble with the operations boss, a married man with two children.

He and his wife were having marital problems and I'm certain it was mostly his fault. Instead of trying to fix things with his wife, he decided to "show her a thing or two" by seeing other women.

There was one young woman in particular he fancied. She worked in the office at Trimfoot. She had been married, had a couple of kids very quickly, and was divorced by the time she was twenty years old. She could be described as "ample" in her womanly physique. The term "top heavy" comes to mind.

Jim, (the operations boss) became abnormally and pathologically fixated on her and he decided to make a play for her.

Let me make it abundantly clear that I did not like her. No one in the office could stand her. She had a voice like Edith Bunker and a laugh like a jackass. If she had an IQ above 25 I would have been greatly surprised. She messed up everything she touched. It was a rare night when I didn't have to fix her coding sheets before giving them to the keypunchers to punch our daily orders.

I approached Jim on a number of occasions

and told him something had to be done about her. Every time I complained, however, he became more angry than before. The situation was creating a lot of bad blood between us.

The final straw came one night when he was on his way out of the office to meet her for drinks. He figured he was finally going to "get lucky" and he told me that if his wife called, I was to tell her that he was somewhere in the warehouse and couldn't be reached.

I couldn't believe my ears. He was telling me to lie to his wife so he could go out and mess around with his little "fixation."

I told him, "No, I won't do that. If you want to lie to your wife, you do it yourself."

His blustered, "Well, why the hell not? I'm not asking you to lie, just tell her I'm unavailable. That's not a lie, is it?"

"I'm not going to cover for you, Jim," I said flatly, "if you want to screw around behind your wife's back, that's your business, but I'm not going to be involved."

He blew up and spewed a stream of hateful, angry words, calling me some highly inappropriate names.

I responded to his vituperative verbiage with an equal amount of profanity and name calling. The keypunch crew sat in the back of the room keeping quiet but enjoying the show.

That's when he threatened to fire me for refusing to follow his orders. I politely informed him that if he fired me, everyone I knew would find out about his duplicitous whoring around;

and the first person on my list would be his wife.

We stood there hating each other until he turned and walked away, cursing me under his breath.

From then on, he never talked to me. He gave directives to me through one of the office girls and I returned his favor in the same manner. I began to make a daily diary of everything that happened on my shift just in case I needed any sort of ammunition to protect myself. From that point on, I've always had the habit of writing a "work diary" for every job I've had until my retirement. As the Boy Scouts say, "Be prepared."

But, as the saying goes, "When one door closes, another opens."

During the summer of 1966, my brother Freddie Lee brought his family from Spring Valley, California for a visit to the Lead Belt.

He, his wife Dorothy, and the two kids, John and Sue Ann stayed with Dorothy's parents, Walter and Sue Cook at 508 South Grant Street in Desloge, Missouri.

The last time I saw them was in 1962, at their house on Old CC Highway just outside of Festus, Missouri.

After basic training at Fort Leonard Wood and a couple of weeks at home, I was scheduled for military training at Fort Benjamin Harrison in Indianapolis, Indiana.

The army had promised to teach me how to operate IBM punch card machines at their Electrical Accounting Machine (EAM) School and

Freddie offered to drive me there. He and his whole clan dropped me off at the barracks, they waved goodbye, and I was on my own. I finished the school, the army sent me to Germany, and I didn't return to American soil until May, 1965.

During his 1966 visit to Desloge, he phoned Grandma Province and she told him where I lived. He stopped by one day and he wouldn't stop talking about how great San Diego was.

I started giving a lot of thought to moving to San Diego. I didn't have a lot to keep me in the Lead Belt and sunny California was beginning to sound pretty good.

Freddie and his family returned to California and I began to make plans for the move to San Diego.

By the middle of 1967, I had finally had enough of Jim and his bullshit. I had been saving what money I could so I sold the house, packed everything I owned into the back of my 1963 Volkswagen, and I headed for Route 66. I was on my way.

It was a long, hard trip; mile after mile, hour after hour, and day after day. I began to feel like one of the Joads from Steinbeck's *The Grapes of Wrath.*

Old Route 66 went through hundreds of small towns I can't even remember. I do remember having to slow down to 25 and sometimes 15 miles-per-hour going through those little burgs to keep from getting stopped by a traffic cop.

There were no McDonalds, no Burger Kings, and no Wendys on Route 66. Each town had its own greasy-spoon café and their own brand of hamburgers and french fries, and they were all better than anything you can get in today's fast food joints.

I drove through Springfield and Joplin in Missouri, through Tulsa, Sapulpa, and Oklahoma City in Oklahoma; through Shamrock, Conway and Amarillo in Texas; through Tucumcari, Gallup, and Truth or Consequences in New Mexico; through Navajo, Winona, Flagstaff, and Oatman in Arizona; finally reaching the California border.

I passed motels built like wigwams, frontier forts, and flying saucers.

I saw signs for "museums" with two-headed snakes, two-headed turtles, mummified babies, alien creatures from outer space, and meteorites.

I couldn't count all the roadside shacks selling petrified wood, quartz crystals, geodes of all kinds, arrowheads, moccasins, "real" indian headdresses, bow-and-arrow sets, Kachina dolls, and pop-guns.

It became a real treat to read the old *Burma-Shave* signs as I passed them on my journey west.

The interstate highways bypass those places now and most of them are ghost towns.

Instead of going through Needles and across California to Los Angeles, I opted for California's Highway 95 to the South. It's often referred to as *the loneliest highway in America* and I can certainly give witness to that.

I kept driving until I encountered Highway 8 where I made a right turn and headed toward San Diego.

Reaching the city limits of San Diego, I pulled over to the side of the road to study my map and I slowly made my way into Spring Valley and onto Enfield Street, looking for 1647.

As I neared the correct house number I slowed down when I noticed Dorothy, John, and Sue Ann sitting out in the front yard, playing with Cuddles. I waved at them and Dorothy just stared as I drove by. She finally yelled out, "Hey, that's Mike!"

I turned into a nearby driveway and made my way back to park in front of their house. We went inside and talked about my trip. She said Fred would be home soon.

She told me to bring my bag into the house and I was given John's room to sleep in. After a couple of days, though, he got his room back when I was transferred to an army cot in the garage and I was fine with that arrangement. I was dry, comfortable, and I didn't want to run John out of his own space. Given my financial state, I was grateful for a clean place to sleep.

When Freddie arrived, we talked some more and then he went out to get supper, which consisted of a variety of Taco Bell entrées.

In 1967, the Taco Bell fast food franchise was a year old. The menu consisted of: Tacos, Tostadas, Burritos (Bean, Beef, or Combo), Enchiritos (Taco Bell's version of an enchilada), Frijoles (now called Pintos & Cheese), and Bell

Burgers (a Tex-Mex Sloppy Joe).

I couldn't help being amused at how Freddie went on and on about how good everything was. He was exceedingly animated as he mentioned, *"And everything on the menu is 19-cents!"* Freddie was always close with a penny and a *19-cent Menu* was close to Nirvana for him.

How close with a penny was he, you might ask. All I can say is one day I saw him take a dollar bill out of his wallet and George Washington was shading his eyes from the sunlight.

We had many meals like that during my stay with them while I searched for a job. Even after I had moved out and found a job, I occasionally spent time there sharing food and laughs.

When I think of those gatherings, sharing the cheapest grub Freddie could find, I always think of Cuddles, the family dog.

We were sitting at the table, having lunch. Freddie had just finished explaining his latest grandiose intrigue for ingratiating himself with local Boy Scout leaders. He never stopped thinking up schemes for self-promotion. He once asked me to write a letter to the Boy Scouts praising him and suggesting that he should receive that year's award for being the Greatest Scout of the Year, or some such thing. It was all a bunch of *hoo-doo*. Freddie never did anything unless it benefited him in some way.

Anyway, like I was saying, we were having lunch when I noticed poor little Cuddles out in the back yard. He was scratching himself, yelping, and jumping into the air. He kept repeating the same actions; scratch, scratch, yelp, jump . . . scratch, scratch, yelp, jump . . . again and again.

I said, "What the heck is Cuddles doing?"

Everybody began to watch him and we became concerned.

We left the table and went to the back yard.

I grabbed Cuddles and held him while John examined him. We were all mystified when he began to laugh.

Dorothy said, "What's so funny?"

John said, "He ate a rubber band and it's sticking halfway out his rear end. When he scratches, he catches it with his toenail, it stretches out and then snaps back against his rear end."

Dorothy said, "Why is he eating rubber bands?"

Freddie said, "Pull it out."

John said, "I'm not gonna touch that thing."

I reached down and pulled on it until it snapped out of poor little Cuddles' butt hole.

Sue Ann said, "Ewww . . . get that away from me," and she ran away.

I let go of Cuddles and he began to run around the back yard, as frisky as ever. He was a happy little dog.

I took the rubber band inside, flushed it down the toilet, and washed my hands.

I said, "I guess I'd better get going. My work here is done," and I started out the front door.

The last thing I heard from inside was

Dorothy saying, "Why is he eating rubber bands?"

Sadly, poor little Cuddles developed health issues in 1970 and was put to sleep. I'll always remember him, though. Every time I see a rubber band, I think of Cuddles. As long as someone remembers you, you're not really gone, are you?

My nephew was always an excellent audience during my visits. I told him lots of stories about my times in the army. He especially liked the one about how my unit, the *65th Data Processing Unit*, got its nickname of *The Commode Commandos*. I'll have to write a story about it sometime. It's a perfect example of how stupid a lot of company commanders are.

I don't remember if I had been living in the garage for three weeks or four weeks when Fred came in one evening and said, "We need to talk."

I said, "Okay. I'm guessing there's something specific *we* need to talk about."

He said, "Yes, there is." He pointed at me and said, "You need to leave."

I said, "Well, it is your house and I don't want to over stay my welcome . . . even though you said I could stay here until I found a job. What exactly is the problem?"

He got a very serious look on his face and said, "Dorothy is uncomfortable with you being out here. She says she doesn't have the freedom she needs with you here. If she wants to come out to the garage, she can't because *you're* here."

When he said she was "uncomfortable" I

thought of Ellen and her complaint. I began to wonder if I was really that difficult to live with.

I just shook my head and said, "Okay. If that's what you want, I'll be out as soon as possible."

After giving it some thought, however, I doubted very much that his request for me to leave had anything to do with Dorothy. Knowing Freddie the way I did, I'm certain he was the one who wanted me out. He was just using Dorothy as an excuse. If I were a betting man, I'd wager that he told her I had decided to leave because of her.

The short time I lived there, I had seen and heard things that I did not like. Freddie always had to be the cock of the walk and I think my presence hampered his style, which was often mean, spiteful, and physically abusive. I had hoped that he might have changed since we were kids, but that didn't happen. He was just an older version of a mean little kid and he still had a rotten streak in him.

As I laid there on the cot, I thought about some of the things he did to both me and Harold when we were little kids. I'm not going to delve into that, though. Let's just say Freddie had one hell of a mean streak in him.

Although he was abusive to both Dorothy and John, I had noticed that he left Sue Ann alone. I never witnessed any evidence of him trying to hurt her in any way. Decades later, John told me that Freddie admitted to him once that Sue Ann reminded him of Mama and that's why he never hit her.

Like I had told him, though, it was his house. I packed up that night, and the next morning, I got into my little VW and left.

Having no where else to go, and with my money running out, I drove to a sleazy motel on El Cajon Boulevard. It was one of those high-class joints where a room could be rented by the hour. I was more interested in the big sign they had out front. It said that if you paid $100 in advance, you could stay in one of their well appointed rooms for a whole month. That was a hell of a lot of money back then, especially to somebody whose bank account was running on fumes. The cockroaches in the rooms were free.

I shelled out the money and immediately went across the street to pick up a newspaper. I had become well acquainted with the employment section of the *Want Ads*. Little did I know that I would eventually work for the company that published the very newspaper I was reading.

I lived there for about two weeks when I got lucky. I interviewed for a computer operator's job at Control Data Corporation. At the time, Control Data was a big competitor of IBM. They had a lot of big money contracts with the Federal Government, Raytheon, and other defense contractors. The company manufactured "big iron" mainframe computers. It was a good job.

I was living on dented cans of unlabeled soup and if it weren't for a Shell credit card, I would have been stranded. I wouldn't have been able to get to the interview for the job I just got. I had even missed a couple of car payments, but I reminded myself, "Things could always be worse."

I went to work, saved every penny I could, and rented a teeny, tiny place at 5127 Muir Avenue in Ocean Beach. It was only a two block walk to the beach and there was a bar on the corner called *Edna's Leilani Club* for weekend entertainment.

I kept in contact with Freddie and his family, but my visits became more and more infrequent. I got tired of watching his abusive tactics, especially against my nephew, John. I eventually just quit going over there.

One Saturday night, I was sitting on a bar stool in the *Leilani Club* thinking about my future. I seemed to be headed nowhere.

I was unaware that in December of 1969 I would get married and in December of 1970 I would become a father. Nor did I expect to find a job at the San Diego Union-Tribune Newspaper, which I did, and that I would be there for almost forty years.

Many things would happen that I never anticipated. Things like getting a degree in Computer Science, teaching in the San Diego Community College system, or writing a bunch of books about World War II, the Korean War, and computer textbooks.

I especially never expected to write a series of books about my childhood in Flat River, Missouri. It's funny how things turn out. Life can be full of surprises.

As I sat there, I realized how drastically my life had changed. Flat River, Missouri was no longer my home.

I had suffered severe heartaches, I had been abused by the Army, and I had grown up. Now, I was embarking on a divergent path beyond my wildest dreams.

I was no longer *A Little Kid From Flat River.*

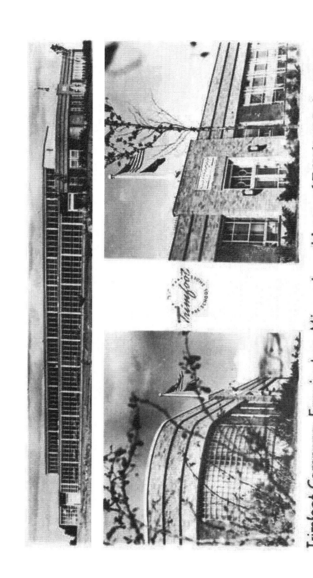

A vintage postcard showing the Trimfoot Company in 1944.

Burma Shave signs were a bright spot for the traveler on old Route 66.

The Rivermines IGA grocery store where I worked for a month before I was fired to make room for the owners niece.

One of the first Taco Bell fast-food joints in California. The sign on the left says it all. Anything on the menu for just 19-cents.

My nephew, John Province on the left; my niece, Sue Ann Province on the right; and poor little Cuddles - the rubber band eating dog - in the front.

Made in the USA
San Bernardino, CA
15 January 2015